ZENITH CITY

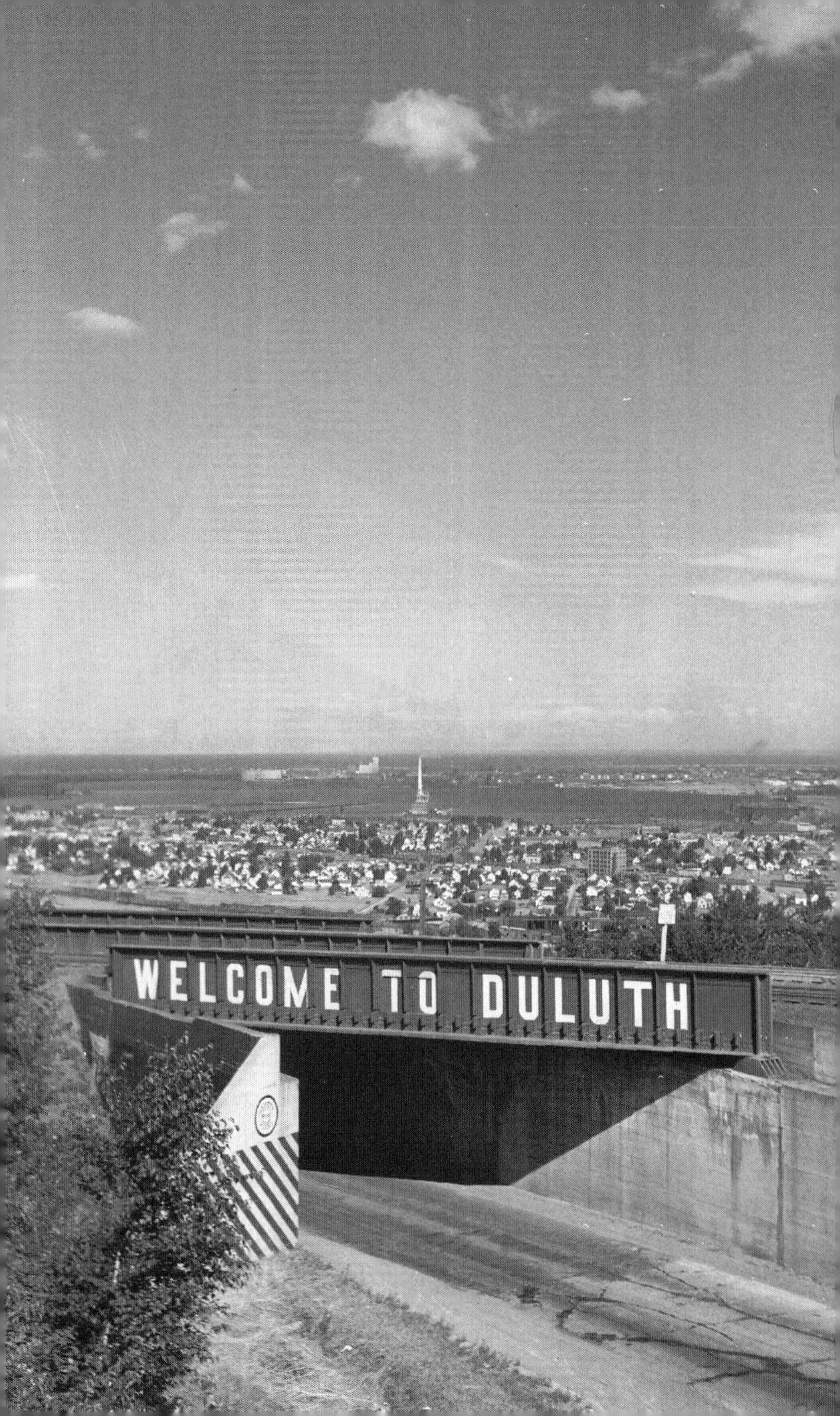
WELCOME TO DULUTH

ZENITH CITY

STORIES FROM DULUTH

Michael Fedo

University of Minnesota Press
Minneapolis
London

Frontispiece: John Vachon, "Entering Duluth, Minnesota," August 1941. Library of Congress Prints and Photographs Division, FSA/OWI Collection.

In several chapters names of persons, living or deceased, have been altered.

For information on previously published material in this book, see pages 175–76.

Copyright 2014 by Michael Fedo

Published by the University of Minnesota Press
111 Third Avenue South, Suite 290
Minneapolis, MN 55401-2520
http://www.upress.umn.edu

Library of Congress Cataloging-in-Publication Data
Fedo, Michael
    Zenith City: stories from Duluth / Michael Fedo.
    ISBN 978-0-8166-9110-4 (pb.)
    1. Duluth (Minn.)—History—Anecdotes. 2. Duluth (Minn.)—
Biography—AnecdotesF .3 .edo, Michael W.—Childhood and youth—
Anecdotes. I. Title.
4102 44F8D.416F
32cd—177´6.779

                                                    8132403102

Printed on acid-free paper

The University of Minnesota is an equal-opportunity educator and employer.

If the immortal spirit of Homer could look down from another heaven than that created by his own celestial genius upon the long lines of pilgrims from every nation of the earth to the gushing fountain of poesy opened by the touch of his magic wand, if he could be permitted to behold the vast assemblage of grand and glorious productions of the lyric art called into being by his own inspired strains, he would weep tears of bitter anguish that instead of lavishing all the stores of his mighty genius upon the fall of Ilion it had not been his more blessed lot to crystallize in deathless song the rising glories of Duluth.

—J. Proctor Knott, 1871

CONTENTS

INTRODUCTION

A WRITER'S MEMORY IS HIS BANK, his repository of narratives that he honestly endeavors to resurrect when writing. Regardless of others' perceptions and recollections, these remain his truth.

While not blessed with total recall, I remember many instances from toddlerhood, like my second birthday, when Dad gave me a baseball glove and delighted in rolling a ball over the living room carpet, urging me to catch it and cheering when the ball bumped the glove. I used to amaze adults in the family by accurately recounting my second Christmas, when I was awakened by bright lights from a neighbor who came to film me opening gifts. I received a fancy pedal-powered car and many other toys, but I was more delighted by a purple balloon and the empty boxes that had contained my presents.

I also possess clear images from the winter day before I turned three, when I rolled down the icy front steps of our duplex on Regent Street. Clad in a maroon snowsuit, I received a deep gash on the bridge of my nose; a faint scar remains visible to this day. Then when I was not yet four, baby brother David suffered a convulsion and Mother sent me downstairs to summon Norma Ranta, an LPN. Mrs. Ranta hurried to our upstairs half of the duplex and, while I watched, helped Mother immerse David in lukewarm water until Dr. Buckley arrived and had David taken to the hospital. My father took me across the street where I spent several days in a yellow two-story house with Aunt Bert and Uncle Charlie Peterson until David's crisis passed. Twenty-five or so years later, their son, my cousin Chuck, would be a featured reed player for the band on the Tennessee Ernie Ford television program.

I hung out in Uncle Charlie's workshop, which was redolent of fresh-shaved wood that he fashioned into children's toys to be sold each Christmas season. I played with Peggy Peterson, the family bulldog.

In later years, Mom and Dad had forgotten that I spent those days with Uncle Charlie and Aunt Bert, who tried one evening to get me to chew an aspirin tablet that she had crushed to stifle the onset of a fever, fearing I might convulse like David. When I refused, Aunt Bert, rather than waste an aspirin, chewed it down herself. Aunt Bert's meatloaf wasn't nearly as good as Mother's or Grandma's, and my aunt had no ketchup to pour on it either. Despite my parents' doubts, these incidents are not only true but vividly so.

And if they had not happened, how could I be remembering them?

I WAS BORN at St. Luke's Hospital in Duluth, Minnesota, on the morning of May 31, 1939, despite the fervent wish of my parents, Ramona and Michael Fedo, that I arrive a day later on June 1 and thereby share the birth date of my father, Michael Anton Fedo. My parents named me Michael Warren Fedo, hoping that with a different middle name I wouldn't be tagged with the moniker Junior. I was called Junior anyway, but not until twenty-three years later when Dad and I both taught at the same time at Denfeld High School. In order to distinguish us, Dad was Fedo Senior and I was Junior, which may have factored into my resignation two years later. No one called Junior exudes gravitas to teens, and I deemed it in my best interest to move on.

My naming was a foretokening of minor confoundings to come, but my parents didn't know that then, nor did I, being only a few hours removed from the womb.

Over the years I've wondered if because I've been alternately called Mickey, Mike, and Michael, without ever totally settling on one, I've struggled, in contemporary parlance, to find myself. Life was a blasé flounder through post–high school years, seeking social diversions instead of devoting time to studying for college classes. An adviser at the University of Minnesota–Duluth insisted I had drifted too long; if I didn't declare a major, I would be denied continued enrollment. I settled on speech only because I had thus far earned B grades in those classes without putting forth much effort. A career in teaching was never envisioned, but that's what I did, simply because there were several offers to teach—and none from Hollywood or major broadcast networks.

I've been told (and I wouldn't argue) that since I never focused on a prospective career, I was like the medieval serf who caught a sack of coins tossed by the prince as he rode through the village, which assured his future. Alas, that practice died centuries earlier, and nobody, let alone benevolent princes, galloped through my town on horseback.

I was well along in my twenties when I began to write. It was not a conscious decision. I'd recently abandoned a stint as a folksinger/comic due to diminishing bookings at clubs and colleges. But when I recounted anecdotes from that sojourn, friends urged me to write them down and send them to a magazine like *Reader's Digest* that might pay a thousand dollars for a story. I wrote a five-page article that *Reader's Digest* promptly returned, sans the one thousand dollars. Several months later a much smaller and now long-defunct publication took the article and paid me sixty dollars.

I had only spent two or three hours on the project while I was in graduate school on a $1,600 per year assistantship. I thought I could write a short article each week and augment my meager salary by selling at least one every month. Prospects seemed bright at the time.

But in fact, though I dutifully crafted my weekly essays, fifteen months passed before another found a home. In the process, however, I developed discipline and became a writer despite receiving only fifty dollars for the second publication.

THE FOLLOWING ESSAYS are true stories as best I recall, and nearly every one of them is situated in or around Duluth, Minnesota. They reflect the people and places that shaped the twenty-five formative years of my residence. For years after, I seemed oblivious to the influence Duluth held over my writing life.

I left the city in August 1964, resigning the position at Denfeld High School and departing the family home at 918 North Tenth

Avenue East, for graduate school at Kent State University in Ohio. I would not live in the city again, assuming domiciles in Kent and Marietta, Ohio; Menomonie, Wisconsin; Peru, New York; and several suburbs of Minneapolis. It wasn't until I began poring over essays written during the more than four decades following my egress that I realized Duluth's people and places permanently inhabit my soul.

More than a third of all my published nonfiction has a Duluth mooring, borne in memory, and surfacing on the printed pages of newspapers and magazines, and online.

Most prominent of the Duluth stories are *The Lynchings in Duluth,* which documented the tragic 1920 hangings of three innocent black men for the alleged and ultimately unproven assault on a young white girl, and the whimsical neighborhood yarns that became *The Chronicles of Aunt Hilma and Other East Hillside Swedes.*

Is there something about Duluth that drives artistic and creative endeavor? The city has apparently fostered those yearnings for a cluster of notables including Nobel laureate Sinclair Lewis; the great jazz pianist Sadik Hakim; popular song lyricist Sammy Gallop; Lorenzo Music, creator of *The Bob Newhart Show* and the voice of Garfield; Bill Berry, former drummer for REM; actress Dorothy Arnold, who was more famous as Joe DiMaggio's first wife; painter David Ericson; Native American artist Carl Gawboy; screenwriters Sidney Buchman (*Mr. Smith Goes to Washington, Lost Horizons,* producer of *The Group*) and Dennis Shryack (*Turner and Hooch, Run,* and others). Popular twentieth-century novelist Margaret Culkin Banning was a longtime resident, essayist and story writer Carol Bly was born here, and the actor Telly Savalas lived in Duluth near the end of his life and did TV commercials for the city, likening it to an inland San Francisco. The 1950s television celebrity, acerbic Henry Morgan, got his professional broadcasting start at radio station WEBC and once said on *What's My Line* that the biggest mistake he'd made in his life was leaving Duluth. My mother graduated from Duluth Central High School with Robert Gilruth, who became one of NASA's leading scientists and who suggested a manned moon shot to John F. Kennedy. Gilruth also headed the Johnson Space Center during the Apollo lunar landings. Duluth proclaimed a Robert Gilruth Day during the late 1960s.

Bob Dylan, of course, was born in Duluth but left for Hibbing when he was only six, so our town is probably entitled to no more than a quarter credit for influencing his ultimate iconography.

Perhaps there was something in the water that spurred demiurgic initiative. Before Lake Superior was befouled by taconite tailings dumped offshore by Reserve Mining, the purity of the lake's water was unquestioned. At the pumping station out along Highway 61, a sign by the outdoor drinking fountain said something like "The Purest Water in the World." In the summer its parking area was filled with out-of-state visitors who stood in line for a refreshing drink. Sport anglers weren't required to carry water on boats; they used a cup to scoop clean, cold water from the lake and gulp it down. Most of Duluth's distinguished creative folk lived there and matured prior to the toxic disposal in the lake.

In the 1940s and 1950s, people came to Duluth to escape ragweed and other pollens, and the city proclaimed itself the hay fever relief capital of the world. Perhaps hay fever inhibited inventive urges elsewhere, whereas its absence encouraged them.

And it may have been the physical beauty of the place. Sinclair Lewis, a conspicuous cynic, quite often rhapsodized over the look of the city on a hill. Perhaps, too, it was the climate; winters especially were grist for storytellers and certainly inspired painters.

MY COUSIN JOHN FEDO served three terms as mayor of Duluth during the late 1980s and early 1990s, but I wasn't there to bask in the family pride over his elections, enjoyed by all of the large Italian Fedo clan, most of whom began their lives in Duluth but had scattered to Detroit, Kansas, California, Florida, and elsewhere at the onset of and following World War II.

There was much in and of Duluth that I took for granted during my tenure. There was the lake, of course, which was always visible from our front yard on Tenth Avenue East, and the concomitant mournful foghorn that I loathed as a kid whenever I heard its "uuun-awww" groan upon waking in the morning. It meant there was a good chance our ballgame would be postponed or canceled— a terrible proposition for a twelve-year-old lover of the game. Now, however, I'm nostalgic for the horn that so often depressed and disappointed me during boyhood.

I even miss the old bowery district between Fifth and Sixth Avenues West on Superior Street. As a youngster selling candy to raise money to buy uniforms or other baseball equipment for the various teams on which I played, I found that the habitués of the old Classy Lumberjack and other denizens my mother warned me to never enter were easy marks in their sundry stages of intoxication. Some might not have 50 cents for a box of Life Savers, but they had a dime or a quarter to give to a youth baseball program. One scruffy patron handed me a quarter and an admonition: "When you're old enough to start dating girls, young fella, take my advice and stay away from the ones that smoke and stay up late."

I DROVE TO CHESTER BOWL on Skyline Drive last summer to wander through my boyhood haunt. Back then the two ponds below the ski jumps allegedly held brook trout, and enhancing the legend, I sometimes saw fly-fishers flicking casts, hoping to lure one. My pals and I would bike up the hill, carrying cheap rods and tins of freshly dug angleworms. We never caught a trout, never even saw one, but on rare occasions my neighborhood buddy Dick Hassinger coaxed a chub or two out of the pool.

There were clay tennis courts and an adjacent field large enough to hold two baseball games simultaneously. A ball hit into Chester Creek was a ground rule double, though even the slowest kid could make a triple out of a ball that didn't quite reach the water. In our games, though, when an opponent smacked a line drive toward the creek and it rolled down the bank, whether the ball hit the water or not, a savvy right fielder, beyond the view of umpires, would kick it into the creek, then show the ump a soggy ball, which sent the disgruntled batter (who may have already made a home run) back to second base.

The Olympic ski jumper Gene Kotlarek got his start on the Chester Bowl ski jumps. He was once featured in *Time* magazine as the nation's premier jumper.

I was never much of a jumper myself, and I think I only went off the smaller of the two jumps a couple of times before deciding I preferred indoor winter sports and concentrated on basketball instead.

OUR FAMILY, EXCEPT FOR DAD, who was raised Catholic, always attended Sunday school and services at Bethel Baptist Church on Eleventh Avenue East and Fourth Street. In those days Baptists were an abstemious lot and seemed drawn to the occasional brouhaha over whether the minister should be granted a raise or how vigorously to impress the evils of alcohol and social dancing on teenagers. Often lovely, caring people were on opposite sides of issues, and the church disassembled many years after I left Duluth, arguing, I think, over whether the congregation should sponsor a soup kitchen for the indigent.

While the church connection here is tenuous, septuagenarian and octogenarian Duluthians will recall painted inscriptions on rock and cliff facings around southern St. Louis County proclaiming "The Lord Is Coming." The most prominent was on the old Point of Rocks, at the convergence of Michigan Street, Superior Street, and Mesaba Avenue. This was the work of our local Jeremiah, Everett Scheall, who called himself "Reverend" though apparently he had not attended a seminary. His ministry consisted of painting the ubiquitous prophecy in white wherever he could. While he wasn't a member of our congregation, his wife and children were regular attendees.

One of my favorite Bethel memories, dating to the early 1960s, occurred near the end of a sermon dealing with declining moral values in society. The minister was especially vexed about the influence rock 'n' roll music held over teenagers, and he excoriated those who performed the music as well as those who habitually listened to it. He concluded by warning the congregation of the unsavory influence of the genre, claiming "God doesn't like that kind of music."

All this being said, I apparently have been able to take leave of Duluth without Duluth taking leave of me. And while my relationship with the city was neither a love fest nor a loathing, it was assuredly tolerable, which is probably how many of us relate to the communities where we were raised.

Most of my Duluth memories are good ones, though these essays may occasionally appear to reflect a lover's quarrel with the city—its seeming insularity during my pubescence that short-circuited dreams of a life beyond Duluth, beyond Minnesota, beyond settling for secure employment before exploring the world at large. I felt that those around me were incapable of nurturing the budding writer I would become; perhaps they believed that should I depart the city I would struggle to earn a living from writing and avoid marriage and begetting the grandchildren desired by my parents. And yet, without my realizing it, my people did nurture me and imparted stories that reside deep in the adytum of my mind, beginning before I entered school, carrying through the two-and-a-half decades I lived in Duluth, and emerging long after I'd left.

I cherish the time in my city and its memories. However, the essayist William Zinsser, in "Writing and Remembering," posits "memory, one of the most powerful of writers' tools, is one of the most unreliable: the boy's remembered truth was often different from his parents' remembered truth."

Does my remembered past differ from my parents' or brothers' memories? Following publication of several essays, one or the other has remarked that my rendering of a family episode was not quite what they recalled. There have been stories that neither one remembers at all. My brother David is four years younger than I, and Stephen is nearly twelve years younger. I suggest neither could be expected to have clear recall on something that transpired when they were very young. That's what I've always told them, and with veiled skepticism they seemed to accept that.

And so it is with these essays. They are my truths, and I'm sticking with them.

THIS IS DULUTH!

It's why we live here in New York, a city that never sleeps,
instead of someplace like Duluth.

—Woody Allen, *Manhattan Murder Mystery*

FOR ALL THE CHUCKLES that line received in the theater where I watched the film, as a native Duluthian it rang true for me. I haven't lived in the city since the mid-1960s, but the effects of national media's frequent lampooning of Duluth reside in my guts and have influenced how I view myself and the world at large.

As a kid growing up in the 1940s and 1950s, our city's sole claim to fame of a sort was the fact that Albert Woolson, the last surviving soldier of the Union Army, resided there. Duluth's only icon, he lived to be 106 or 107 years old. But my hometown's history is replete with stories that fed our collective inferiority, Woody Allen notwithstanding.

In the summer of 1871, when the golden age of piracy had been over for nearly a century, buccaneers pillaged the Duluth harbor. Ships, sawmills, and warehouses were laid waste, and between plunders the latter-day corsairs holed up in a cave on the waterfront. Larger than some oceans, Lake Superior was virgin territory for Henry Morgan, Jean Laffite, or Sir Francis Drake wannabes, who may have been influenced by a July 4, 1868, address in which Dr. Thomas Preston Foster, founder of the city's first newspaper, called Duluth "the Zenith City of the unsalted seas."

Fortunately, the pirates' reign of terror lasted only weeks before their capture by an irate lumberman whose warehouse had been raided. What the pirates may have felt about being captured by a

1

businessman remains speculative, as does the prospect of the male-factors being forced to walk the plank to be pecked by roving schools of lake trout and whitefish.

It is not known if pirates concerned Daniel Greysolon, Sieur du Luth, for whom the city was named, when he crossed the high seas from France to Canada in 1675, as there is no verification of his encountering brigands. Greysolon was born in 1650 to a family of lesser nobility in St. Germain-en-Laye, near Paris. He was appointed to the Garde du Roi under Louis XIV, fought against William of Orange in the Netherlands in 1674, and would doubtless have ac-quitted himself admirably had pirates vexed his journey.

The city of Duluth would take the explorer's title nearly 180 years after he became the first white man to document his arrival there on June 27, 1679. But it wasn't until November 1965 that the city commemorated this valorous adventurer and fur trader with a monument.

In 1675 the French military sent Greysolon to Montreal, but an unhappy love affair in 1678 saw the officer volunteer for a westward excursion to increase France's influence in the expanding fur trade. The next year he landed on what is now Minnesota Point—a long, narrow peninsula between Lake Superior and the St. Louis Bay.

The esteem of Duluth's namesake seems largely established by his alleged rescue of Father Louis Hennepin in 1680, after the priest had been captured by a Dakota tribe. Greysolon had met men who told about abundant salt a twenty-day ride west of what is now Min-nesota. Hoping to discover a passage to the Indies, he set off, unaware of the existence of Great Salt Lake. Shortly after getting underway, he learned of the priest's abduction and, according to local legend, determined to effect a rescue. With his brother Claude and three other men, he pursued 1,100 Dakota for two days and nights, then angrily demanded and secured Father Hennepin's release. Histori-ans, however, completely dispute this account, as it isn't verified by Father Hennepin's diaries; in fact, the priest and his entourage were well treated. Further, the story rings false on the face of it: five men prevailing over more than a thousand Dakota? For whatever reason, Greysolon abandoned his quest for salt and a shortcut to the Indies, and, so goes the old myth, escorted Father Hennepin to safety.

Local and regional histories have little to say about Greysolon, though pioneer civic leaders in the city of Duluth claim the man's reputation would have been greatly enhanced had he not been such a modest, unassuming sort. If true, these attributes were precursors to shaping the characters of Duluthians yet unborn, who grew up believing that it was not only in bad taste but sinful to exalt or reveal oneself.

According to one Duluth-originated legend about its namesake, supernumeraries of the king attempted to dissuade the explorer from undertaking a particularly dangerous mission. Greysolon reportedly responded, "I fear not death—only cowardice and dishonor."

By 1682 Greysolon had returned to France, accused of consorting with the English and mishandling funds. Though acquitted of the charges, his modest fortune was depleted, and Greysolon, who never married, died on February 25, 1710.

A contributor to the book *The History of Duluth and St. Louis County, Past and Present* summed up Greysolon's life and career with fulsome extravagance: "Unselfish, honest, brave beyond the ordinary man, so much so that had some of his deeds been done in the days of Greece or Rome they would have commanded the genius and skill of the greatest artists and sculptors in commemorating them on canvas or marble."

In November 1908, 229 years after Greysolon's Minnesota expedition, the Greysolon Dulhut Memorial Association was formed with the purpose of contracting with a noted sculptor to craft a statue of Greysolon for the city. Bishop of the Duluth Archdiocese, James McGolrick, urged the committee to commission Auguste Rodin for the work. The bishop rhapsodized about Rodin's career as he lectured the committee concerning the French master's qualifications to create the monument. "The studio of M. Rodin on the slopes of Mendon, is the center of attraction for all who love art, from the king to the beggar. . . . The great master . . . is now the Michelangelo of the twentieth century. . . . This is the great artist who is anxious to give as one of the last works of his life artistic expression to the figure of Greysolon DuLhut, a noble subject for his chisel. Can we not enlist the cooperation of all our people in a worthy project? All the more because Rodin himself so heartily approves."

Twenty years later, in 1928, funds to commemorate Greysolon were made available by a local entrepreneur–banker, Albert L. Ordean, who bequeathed $50,000 to the city for a memorial. The long-dormant memorial association began searching for a suitable site on which the statue could be displayed. Alas, Rodin was no longer in the picture, having had the misfortune of dying in 1917 without submitting sketches of Greysolon, denying posterity what chauvinistic Duluthians believed would be his greatest monument. Thus a bereft art world is left to assess Rodin's career solely on such masterpieces as *The Burghers of Calais, The Gates of Hell, The Thinker,* a bust of Victor Hugo, and *The Kiss.*

Without Rodin the project stalled until 1953, when the Park Point American Legion Post urged a statue be commissioned and erected near the Duluth ship canal where the explorer first touched land.

By 1956 the Ordean fund had grown to nearly $80,000. Ignoring the Legion post and suggestions from scores of citizens, trustees of the fund recommended the statue be housed on the campus of the University of Minnesota–Duluth. This seemed, at long last, to get the ball rolling.

The remaining significant issue, however, was what Greysolon looked like. Despite his lifetime achievements as a soldier, explorer, and trader, no copy of his likeness existed. The noted sculptor Jacques Lipschitz was selected by administrators of the trust to imagine a visage of Greysolon for a $77,000 fee. In June 1963, Lipschitz submitted a sketch that was accepted by university regents. The statue would be nine feet high, mounted on a fifteen-foot granite column. Lipschitz fashioned Greysolon in a buckskin jacket and plumed hat. Almost fifty-seven years after the original committee met to discuss raising a monument to Greysolon, the Lipschitz work was unveiled on November 5, 1965.

Person-on-the-street inquiries produced varied reactions, but a plurality suggested that the sculpture resembled a cartoon character. Responding to published remarks that the statue appeared to be "a Disneyesque giant" or a combination of "Cyrano de Bergerac and the Three Musketeers," Lipschitz said, "No one knows what

Sieur duLuth looked like. I had to create an image. To my mind, he belonged to the epoch of the Three Musketeers."

In the years that followed, few would regard the piece charitably, with some Duluthians even suggesting that Lipschitz snookered the city, foisting a second-rate work on them and getting away with it because our backwater rubes wouldn't know any better. A recent student handbook at the University of Minnesota–Duluth, where the figure presides over the Ordean Court plaza, made this observation: "The statue . . . looks like the Michelin Man holding a hot dog and missing his yo-yo."

Most published guides for tourists visiting the city omit mentioning the Lipschitz monument to Daniel de Greysolon, Sieur Du Lhut.

THE BIRTH OF THIS CITY attracted little attention in the early 1850s, more than a century and three-quarters after Greysolon beached his canoe on Minnesota Point, where the present-day Canal Park and Aerial Lift Bridge are situated.

There were only a handful of residents in what would become Duluth until the La Pointe treaty of 1854 with the Ojibwe, which moved the natives further west and south. As far back as 1855, with the opening of a canal at Sault Ste. Marie, Michigan, men exuded confidence in Duluth's future—a confidence that would prove mostly unwarranted. Railroads looked to link the city with both coasts; Duluth would be the only port with rail access to the Atlantic and Pacific oceans.

By 1868 there were still fewer than one hundred residents in Duluth, but the population surged to more than three thousand two years later, owing to investments by robber baron financier Jay Cooke. Cooke picked Duluth as the terminus for the Northern Pacific Railroad, and a prosperous future was anticipated. In 1869–70, Duluth was the fastest-growing city in the country, and its population was expected to overtake Chicago in only a few short years.

The mood of a city on the rise was captured by Moses Armstrong when he visited Duluth in July 1871. He recounted meeting local grain dealers, "a jolly set of men. They are blessed with the happiest wives, the handsomest daughters, and the largest crops of any state in the Union. Many of them were exchanging their new wheat in the sack for old rye in the bottle. The ladies at dinner called for trout and huckleberries, and the tables were so crowded that I was obliged to throw a biscuit at a waiter girl to induce her to bring me a cup of coffee. A wheat buyer told me it was a waste of grain to throw bread at a Duluth girl."

Optimism abounded until Cooke's empire crashed with the stock market in 1873, and Duluth almost disappeared. Its city designation was terminated on March 12, 1877, when the last meeting of the city council was held, and it reverted to village status. By 1881 the economy boomed again without an infusion of Jay Cooke funds, and reaching 35,000 residents by 1887, the village became a city once more.

In 1921 a monument was erected commemorating Cooke, whose tainted reputation could hardly be said to compare with that of the estimable Greysolon. It is located on Ninth Avenue East and Superior Street, across from Leif Erikson Park and a replica of the sailing vessel that transported Viking sailors to the New World. The Cooke statue, popularly known as "A Man and His Dog," occupies a prominent place in Duluth; the effort to honor Greysolon would languish for more than a half century.

"DULUTH! LOVE IT OR LOATHE IT, you can never leave it or lose it." So begins Gore Vidal's 1983 novel, *Duluth*. The geographic Duluth depicted by Vidal is set in the tropics and turns the immoderate climate of my Minnesota hometown 180 degrees. Vidal's observation nonetheless resonates with natives who espouse a kind of self-deprecation about our city and ourselves.

Perhaps this sense of subordination dated back to the infamous stiffing of the Duluth Merritt family by New Yorker John D. Rockefeller. The Merritts are credited with discovering the iron ore pits that for generations enriched mine owners and contributed importantly to the state's economic well-being.

After their 1888 discovery, the Merritts mapped out 500 square miles of mineral-laden land. But they had difficulty getting their ore to markets. Rockefeller watched and waited while the brothers built railroad and loading docks, efforts that seriously stretched their finances. By 1893, creditors were clamoring for payments, and the Merritts offered to sell their holdings to Rockefeller, who owned the local railroad service, for $40 per share. He declined; their situation worsened, and Rockefeller offered to buy at $10 per share, or $900,000, an offer the Duluthians were unable to turn down. For less than $1 million, the East Coast magnate bought nearly $330 million worth of iron ore. Even if old John D. didn't laugh up his sleeve over his triumph, it remained a chicken bone in the throat of Duluthians and helped solidify our sense of resigned, if not genetic, subservience. Of course we and our ilk would be bested by a Rockefeller. And what business did any of us have in thinking we could compete at that level with a New Yorker, no less?

A CHAUVINISTIC THREAD runs throughout a 1950 book titled *This Is Duluth,* by Dora Mary MacDonald, longtime public relations director for the Duluth Board of Education. For more than twenty years Mrs. MacDonald contributed a weekly article about what was going on in Duluth schools for the Sunday Cosmopolitan pages of the *Duluth News Tribune.*

Typical of Mrs. MacDonald's prose is this assessment of the city's character: "The voice of Duluth has a vigorous ring resounding from lake to rock-bound hills, a voice embodying the spirit of the hardy men and women who founded the community. Here is a lusty city, but a city that has its dreams and the capacity to make those dreams come true."

Mrs. MacDonald also discusses the infamous lynchings of 1920, when a large mob hanged three black circus workers on a downtown street corner. She devotes fewer than three hundred words to the tragedy, concluding her brief treatment, "Duluthians prefer not to hear the rattle of the skeleton in the closet. They dwell upon the worthwhile aspects of the city's history and future."

One of those worthwhile aspects occurred recently, when eighty-three years after the murder of those three innocent men the city commissioned and erected a monument to the victims across the street from where they were hanged. The ceremony dedicating the three bronze figures received international press coverage because Duluth was the first U.S. city to have its mayor and city council acknowledge such a crime.

But Dora Mary MacDonald could not have foreseen that. Her Duluth expunged the lynchings from schoolroom discussions, destroyed records and news clips, hoping that future generations would not probe the archives to reexpose Duluth's darkest hour. *This Is Duluth* closes, "It is a city that meets its adversities with courage and clings to its dreams with stubborn tenacity. Poised on its hills it gazes out to the lake, figuratively puts its hand on its hips, raises its chin and cries out to the world, 'What next? We're ready.'"

But we weren't, really. The anticipated economic boom following the opening of the St. Lawrence Seaway fizzled, only adding a few dozen longshoremen and tugboat captains to employment rolls. Far from becoming another Chicago, as local politicians and business leaders optimistically projected, we remained what we had always been—a remote community separated from centers of culture and sophistication, generating in those of us who came of age in the 1950s and 1960s an urge to absent ourselves from the old hometown.

Thus a more appropriate conclusion to Mrs. MacDonald's tome would have been, "We're waiting."

My generation, at least, seemed always to be waiting: waiting to grow up, waiting to graduate from high school, and waiting to depart Duluth.

MISS WEDDEL
AND THE RATS

THOUGH OUR FAMILY LIVED UPSTAIRS in a Regent Street duplex only until I was five, the image of Miss Weddel, who lived next door, remains fixed in my memory seven decades later. A spinster schoolteacher, Miss Weddel's appearance reflected what one might assume a Miss Weddel to look like: pale complexion, severe unsmiling countenance, black hair pulled back into a bun. She wore dresses of black or navy blue, and her hats (always with the veil down) were also black or navy blue.

Her large two-story house was white, surrounded by a three-foot wrought iron fence with a latched front gate. Neighborhood children understood we were under no circumstance to set foot in her yard. Jimmy P. Ames (he always used his middle initial when referring to himself), older than I, who lived across the street, once said he'd gone into her yard to retrieve a ball and Miss Weddel called his parents and threatened to summon (her word) the police should he do so again. Though she interacted with elementary pupils every day, it was clear to everyone in the neighborhood that she disdained children.

On another occasion she upbraided Jimmy because his dog, Fritz, whizzed against her fence. It was widely known that kids did not knock on her door at Halloween. Her imperiousness extended to adults as well as children, and the only time I recall her stepping into our yard was to castigate my father for flooding the large garden space in the backyard so kids on the block had a skating rink. I was there and heard him address her as Miss Weddel, as did all the neighbors, assuring her that the youngsters would not enter her yard.

"Children are so very noisy, you know," she said, not able to discourage him from building and maintaining the rink.

"They're kids, Miss Weddel," he said firmly, and she retreated to her home.

Not long after that exchange, Jimmy P. Ames and I were scuffling along the Regent Street curb in front of our house, when Jimmy spied a large, frozen-stiff rat, the victim of a passing car, in the gutter. It looked scary with its teeth bared. Jimmy poked it with a stick. "Big one," he said, pushing it with his foot.

This wasn't the first rat I'd seen. Our middle-class neighborhood in Duluth's east end harbored rodents, and often when kids gathered outside for play, one would announce that somebody's dad had caught one in a basement trap the night before. I sometimes saw Dad empty a trap holding a dead rat into the trash container. Once in a while, we saw brown rats of varying sizes hanging out around sewers. Sometimes we chucked stones or sticks at them.

Jimmy was studying this rat, however. He stomped on it, which didn't alter the frozen carcass. He spit on it and told me to do the same. Then he had an idea.

"Mickey, I'll open Miss Weddel's gate and you take this rat and put it on her porch."

I obeyed, grabbing the rat by the tail and marching toward Miss Weddel's gate, which Jimmy, laughing now, had unlatched. He waited on the sidewalk as I trudged up the steps and dropped the carcass on the porch.

"Move it close to the door," Jimmy said, and I obeyed again, prodding it atop the mat beneath Miss Weddel's doorbell.

"We better run," Jimmy said, dashing away so fast that I knew I could never catch up. So I let myself out through the gate without latching it and returned to our apartment.

Some time later, perhaps an hour or so—being only four years old then, I couldn't tell time—Mother looked out the window and saw a police car in front of Miss Weddel's house. "Golly," she said, "I hope nothing's wrong over there."

A few weeks later, when our duplex was put up for sale, a prospective buyer was going to stop by for a look. Because the landlord had another appointment at the same time, he asked Mother to show the buyer around. Mother agreed, and when the man arrived, she began his tour, with me in tow. The Rantas had recently moved, so the downstairs was vacant. I recall almost nothing of his inspection of both units, but indeed I remember our trip to the basement.

As we stepped into the dank, darkened, gloomy cellar, Mother snapped on the lights. As the man looked around, I said, "Here's where the rats live."

I think my comment was the deal breaker.

THE ROOMER

FROM OCTOBER 1944 until I departed Duluth, my family lived in a two-story white house on Tenth Avenue East and Tenth Street. Occupying the house next door on our north side was my maternal grandmother, Augusta Norquist, her unmarried daughter Ada, and Hilma Norquist, Grandma's sixty-something spinster sister-in-law.

The homes, which had been built by Mother's father, Eric, were virtually identical. Each featured an enclosed front porch—an extended drawing room at Grandma's house, but a repository for bicycles, camping gear, and athletic paraphernalia at our house.

The houses shared a common driveway, which separated them, and a single-car wooden garage. None of the Norquist women drove, however, so for all intents and purposes, it was our garage. The only Norquist who ever parked in the driveway was Mother's older brother, Howard, who invariably left his car there at the precise moment Dad had to hurry out to a meeting or a rehearsal for the Duluth Symphony, of which he was a charter member. While I'm probably exaggerating somewhat here, I recall that whenever Howard parked in the driveway and Dad had to dash off somewhere, Howard's car refused to start. Howard would always tell Dad that as far as he was concerned, our driveway was a jinx on his car; it never gave him a speck of trouble anywhere else but would always shut down when he parked in our driveway. He just couldn't understand it, he always said. Just as regularly, Dad would say that he didn't care if Howard understood it or not and he should park his damn jalopy in the street from then on. And maybe the next time Howard visited, he would. But the car never failed to start when parked in the street, and sure enough, subsequent visits found Howard's old Chevy stuck in the driveway again.

The business of Howard's car parked in our driveway formed the foundation of Dad's relationship with his brother-in-law, though he never said anything to Grandma, for fear of hurting her feelings, nor to Hilma, who often found Howard's antics irritating—Dad's complaining about Howard would only give Hilma more fodder to use when ragging on poor Grandma, as gentle and kindly a soul as God breathed life into.

Throughout the 1940s, Grandma rented out the spare upstairs bedroom of her house to students, salesmen, or itinerant laborers. At times the room was vacant for weeks on end, since prospective roomers had to pass modest muster imposed by Grandma, who insisted that no liquor be brought onto the premises and that there be no smoking in the rented room except with the door closed.

Getting past Aunt Hilma was another matter. Though Grandma owned the house, Hilma retained certain rights as she had forsaken a career and marriage to care for my grandfather's aged parents. Eric Norquist, before he died, had made it clear that Hilma was to always have a home with his family because of her selflessness.

A severe woman with a firmly set mouth, Hilma's brown-gray hair was always tied back in a bun. She wore black linen dresses and a green wool sweater summer and winter. Hilma was opposed not only to smoking and drinking but to frivolous laughter and members of the Lutheran church. She turned down one man for being Lutheran. "Da Lutrans make a big show of church on Sundays, but da rest of da veek, vatch out." Hilma, who was the only member of her Swedish clan born in America, nonetheless had the thickest Scandinavian accent of her surviving sisters.

Now and again, when Hilma happened to be downtown or working as a seamstress at Garon's Mill in West Duluth, Grandma would accept a man without Hilma's approval. Then Hilma would sulk and keep to her room for several days, emerging only to eat well after Grandma and Ada had eaten.

In time, however, she'd come to accept the new roomer if he caused no trouble. This did not mean she would speak to him, and, in fact, she never to my recollection spoke directly to a roomer. If she had a complaint, as she often did—"Da roomer used up all da hot vater" or "I seen some filty magazines on his bed"—my peace-loving grandmother tried to soothe her. If unsatisfied with Grandma's efforts, Hilma would approach my father to deal with the malefactor.

Dad always asked what Hilma would have him say to the roomer, which incensed her. "Vat do you tink you should say?" she'd ask crossly. "Uff. If I vas a man, I'd see to it he got plenty of trouble." And Dad would agree to at least talk to the man.

I remember when a roomer named Edward was leaving and gave Grandma two weeks' notice. She placed a small ad in the newspaper and waited for responses. There were none, and she anticipated a lengthy wait before filling the room. Rarely dismayed at this prospect, for it had happened before, this time she wanted to send twenty-five dollars to the Baptist church to kick off the new building fund. The money would be available only if the room were rented.

Edward, learning of the difficulty Grandma was having in replacing him, told her of an acquaintance at work who might be looking for a new place. Edward said he'd talk to the fellow and have him stop by for an interview.

Edward had been tolerated rather well by Hilma, as he was not a mirthful man. In his late twenties, he wore dark horn-rimmed glasses and was memorable for his prodigious appetite. The only meal he took at Grandma's was breakfast, which never varied. It consisted of an entire box of cold cereal emptied into a large mixing bowl and topped with most of a quart of milk.

Edward's acquaintance was named Stiles—I never caught his first name. He arrived with his gear on a Saturday morning, shortly after Hilma had boarded a bus for downtown. Grandma may have been uneasy about taking him, but Stiles told her he had no place else to go and was counting on getting that room. He apologized for not being able to pay more than a week in advance, but he was steadily employed, and said he understood the house rules. He would be no bother.

With some hesitation, Grandma took him to the room and let him bounce a time or two on the bed. He checked the closet and said he'd take the room. Then he handed Grandma seven one-dollar bills and left to attend to some errands.

Hilma returned about noon, and Grandma told her about the new roomer. Hilma was skeptical, reminding Grandma that the last time Grandma had accepted a roomer without her consent, the bounder had left town owing two weeks' rent.

About three o'clock, Stiles returned, said nothing, and went upstairs.

Perhaps an hour later, Hilma went to her room for a sweater, only to find Stiles in her bed. She was mortified, for not only was a stranger beneath her covers, but she discovered he'd also failed to negotiate his way to the bathroom down the hall. He had thrown up on her lamp stand.

Hilma stomped downstairs, angry tears spurting from her eyes. "Gustie," she snarled in a hoarse whisper. "Da new man is drunk in *my* bed. He womited and da room stinks."

Grandma slowly wiped her hands on her white apron. "Maybe the poor fellow is sick."

"He's drunk. Trew up in my room. How are we going to get him out of dere, Gustie?"

"Mike will talk to him," Grandma said. She turned to me. I was in her kitchen, downing my fourth ginger cookie. "Mickey, bring your daddy over here right away, will you? Tell him we've got a little trouble with the new roomer."

"Tell him ve got lots of trouble," Hilma harrumphed. "I tell you, I'm so mad I could yust spit."

I bounced across the twelve-foot driveway. Dad was in the basement working on the washing machine. "Grandma says they got trouble with the roomer," I said.

Dad grimaced. "What's up?" He wiped his hands on a chamois cloth.

"I think he's drunk and threw up in Hilma's room."

Dad let a long sigh escape his lips. He started up the stairs and crossed the driveway with me at his heels.

"Mike, he's stinking drunk," cried Hilma as we stepped into the front porch. The summer sun had heated it to more than ninety degrees. My father, already perspiring from his efforts to wrench an ill-tempered motor from our washer, sought the comfort of Grandma's shaded parlor to hear her story.

But Hilma already had her bony, arthritic fingers clamped around his wrist. "You've yust got to get him to leave, Mike. He's in *my* bed." She clutched Dad at both elbows as he entered the house. "Even if he says he'll pay a hundred dollars, ve von't have him." She tried to usher Dad up the stairs.

Dad eased free of her grasp and approached Grandma. "I'll see what I can do," he said, and Grandma shook her head.

"He could be ill, Mike," she offered.

"He's drunk," growled Hilma from the staircase landing.

Dad sighed again. "Stay here," he told me, and ascended the stairs. I could hear only muffled voices from my vantage point below, owing to Hilma's angry expositions to Grandma.

Several minutes later Dad came down. "He'll be gone soon. You gotta be careful about who you let in your house, Grandma."

"Dat's vat I say," Hilma affirmed. "You can say dat again." She blew into her lace hankie.

There was some clamoring at the top of the staircase and Stiles descended, struggling with a seaman's duffel bag. Rumpled and red-faced, he looked at no one, thus escaping Hilma's withering glare. No one moved to help him with the door, and he cursed softly as he managed to get it open before barging out into the late afternoon. He hoisted the bag to his shoulder, hawked and spit into Tenth Avenue, and started unevenly down the hill.

"Thanks a million, Mike," Grandma said. "Will you stay for coffee?"

"No, I don't think so."

"Mike," Hilma started, "you should have thought to have him clean up da mess. I'm mad as a hen about it." She grabbed a dishpan and cloth and started up the stairs. "Dat's the last vun, Gustie. No more roomers." She went up and seconds later wailed, "Oh, noo-ooo."

Dad, from the foot of the stairs called, "What's wrong, Hilma?"

"Da stupid skunk vet my bed too," she sobbed and slammed her door.

Dad threw me a faintly amused glance, and we hurried upstairs to aid Hilma. We found my great aunt ripping bedding from the mattress and, with remarkable strength for a woman so frail in appearance, she removed the mattress from the spring and shoved it out the front bedroom window, where it rested on the roof of the porch. Composing herself then, she went back downstairs, where Grandma said, "You know, he paid for the whole week. You don't suppose we should try to give him back his money, do you?"

A guttural eruption escaped Hilma's throat, and she gripped the sides of the kitchen table. "You're nuts, Gustie."

"I'm sure he didn't mean no harm."

"No harm? No harm? Womit and pee, you call dat no harm?" Hilma sat; her breaths came in labored gasps. "Gustie, you're lucky it vasn't your bed he messed, dat's all I can say."

I left the house then and started back across the driveway to our house. Uncle Howard had just pulled into the drive and was standing by his 1937 Chevy. The hood was up and a great hissing of steam was shooting out of his radiator. He stepped away from the car when he saw me. "Well, Mickey, I wasn't going to drop in today, but I was in the neighborhood when this durned old buggy started acting up. Listen, don't say nothing to your dad, okay? Shoot, she'll start up fine once she cools down."

Later that evening, when Dad was in his usual hurry to get to the symphony concert at the Armory, he got grease smudges on his tux from having to help Howard push the Chevy out of the driveway.

SCHOOL DAYS

TWENTY-FIVE YEARS AGO Robert Fulghum's book *All I Really Need to Know I Learned in Kindergarten* hit the best-seller lists and stayed there for two years. You may recall his lessons: honesty, sharing, showing kindness, cleaning up after yourself, balancing work, play, and learning, among others. I wonder if that book could have been written, or if its conceit would have taken a vastly different direction, had Fulghum attended kindergarten with my lifelong chum Ralph Golberg.

About three weeks into the 1944 school year, our family moved from Regent Street in Duluth's east end to a house next door to my grandmother's on Tenth Avenue East in the Central Hillside neighborhood. I transferred from Lakeside Elementary to U. S. Grant after the move and was immediately aware of Ralph.

He was continually reprimanded for various infractions—talking, poking another child, standing when he was supposed to be sitting, or sitting when ordered to stand. He perpetually got up the nose of Miss Geddes, our elderly teacher.

One morning there was an all-school assembly in the gymnasium, across the hall from the kindergarten classroom. The program was an appeal to children's patriotism during World War II, and we were urged to save our pennies and nickels and dimes to buy war savings stamps. Following the presentation, Mr. Anderson, the principal, dismissed pupils back to their classrooms.

Leaving the gym, I was positioned near Ralph, who spied Mr. Anderson, a tall bald man with a fringe of white hair, motioning children to move along and not make noise as they returned to class.

As Mr. Anderson moved farther down the hall, Ralph piped, "Hey, Baldy," which made me giggle, and I repeated his "Hey, Baldy" myself, only to feel the dry fingers of Miss Geddes clamped on the nape of my neck. She had Ralph's neck in her other hand and hastily marched the two of us back into our room, where in front of the entire class she upbraided us for our "rude, very bad behavior." While Ralph was nonplussed, I was terrified and near tears. Finally Miss Geddes said, "You boys go up to Mr. Anderson's office right this minute and tell him what you did. You will tell him you are very, very sorry." She led us to the door and ushered us into the hall. I immediately started for the stairs leading to the principal's second-floor office. I had begun to cry, fearing retribution from the principal and certain my parents would be notified of my transgression.

Ralph sauntered toward the drinking fountain, pausing to glance at me. "Where are you going?"

"Teacher said we—we have to go to the office." I turned and started back up the stairs.

"We're not going," Ralph said, his voice firm, insistent.

I panicked. "What will we do?"

Calmly and confidently he replied, "We'll walk around in the hall for a few minutes and go back in."

"Yeah, but what if she—?" I choked on a frightened sob.

"If she asks what we said, we'll tell her we told him we were sorry. And," he added emphatically, "if she asks us what he said, we'll say he told us to never do that again." He leaned over the fountain and drank.

Still terrified, both of Miss Geddes and of Ralph's boldness, I walked around the hall with him for several minutes. Ralph, however, retained his nonchalance, pausing to look at pupils' artwork posted in the hallways, chuckling at some pieces and making derisive comments about others.

Finally we returned to our room, and precisely as five-year-old Ralph predicted, Miss Geddes asked us what transpired. "We told him we were sorry," Ralph said.

"And what did Mr. Anderson say?"

"He told us never to do it again."

"Very well," said Miss Geddes. "See to it that you don't. I hope you've learned your lesson here. Now quietly take your places in the circle."

What I learned from Ralph that morning was that some children had moxie even at a tender age, and while the values espoused by Robert Fulghum endure, in some circumstances they can be trumped by chutzpah.

NEAR THE END OF SUMMER in 1962, I was graduating from the University of Minnesota–Duluth with a BS in speech education and awaiting my first faculty orientation as instructor of tenth-grade English at Duluth Denfeld High School. My assignment to teach English was something of a surprise as I had only an English minor, with little academic grounding in rules of grammar.

An advance copy of the English 10 curriculum revealed a unit with strong emphasis on grammar, for which I was not prepared, nor was there time for me to embark on a crash course. Ruing my inadequacy, I offhandedly mentioned this to Orlo Anderson, who taught in Denfeld's business department. "Not a big deal," he said. "There'll be kids in your classes who already know that stuff. Get one of them to teach the unit."

"You mean just get some kid up front to teach?"

"Nah," Orlo said. "Ask a question, like 'Who knows what such-and-such is?' Some kid'll know, and you're off the hook."

During the first week of class I discovered James, a bright engaging chap who had been drilled in grammar by nuns in the Catholic school he'd attended from grades one through eight. And as luck would have it, he was in my first-period class.

On the day we were to begin the grammar unit, I said, "Most of you have done some sentence diagramming in junior high. But we need to refresh your skills. James, would you please step to the board and diagram the following sentences . . . ?"

James diagrammed, and I recorded his examples to use in the rest of that day's classes. James was also fluid in explaining gerunds, nominative case, subjunctive mode, and, in fact, all modes, cases, and clauses. Orlo Anderson's suggestion served me well.

Many, if not most, teachers have at times relied on subterfuge in problem solving. Long before I began my career at Denfeld, Ray Ignatius, my old gym teacher and coach at Washington Junior High, had an ingenious approach to disciplining pupils who engaged in fisticuffs on school property. At the time none of the students were aware of the creative stratagem he employed when dealing with boys who brawled. Many on the faculty who broke up a fracas never marched offenders to the principal's office but instead sent them to Ray in the gym after school, where he had the boys drag out mats and don boxing gloves. Ray would blindfold them, saying when he blew his whistle they were to start swinging. When they heard the second whistle they were to immediately stop. He'd turn each kid around several times, then blow his whistle.

After the turning, combatants were often separated by several yards. While they'd harmlessly flail, Ray would slip on a pair of gloves and administer a couple of pops to each one, remove and put away his own gloves, let the bout continue several more seconds, then blow his whistle. Recidivism was almost nonexistent during Ray's three-decade tenure.

The practice wouldn't be tolerated today, and it may not have been back in the '50s and '60s either—but mum was the word. When a former classmate returned to teach at Washington, he learned of Ray's "discipline," which he recounted to me at a class reunion sometime after Ray's passing.

I should add that Ray could also discombobulate pupils. We weren't allowed to put street shoes in the gym's lockers, so they were left on the floor beneath benches in front of the lockers. One morning after our seventh-grade class, a scrawny kid tapped Ray's shoulder and said that someone had taken his left shoe, leaving behind a right shoe of similar shape and color. "What am I supposed to do?" he asked. Not missing a beat, Ray said, "Should be easy to find him in the hall. He'll be walking in circles to his left and you'll walk in circles to your right. Eventually you'll bump into each other."

FRANK WAS NOT officially an educator. He was a night custodian at Washington, a squat bulldog man of middle age. What he imparted was not wisdom or life skills but demonstrations of imprecation extremis. Not before or since have I encountered anyone so foul of mouth. Most likely he was assigned night duties to keep students from hearing (and perchance emulating) his vile oaths. While a milder sort might have whistled or hummed when performing routine tasks, Frank swore, a constant stream of rages varying from raspy rumbles to ear-piercing shrieks when he was steamed. And when he was, he could be heard on floors above and below where he worked.

I and other student athletes would finish our practice sessions about a half hour after Frank arrived on duty. He singed our virgin ears with diatribes we never imagined. Walking down from the fourth-floor gymnasium, we could hear Frank as he swept or mopped a room, his voice sharp, ascending as he cursed his equipment, the rooms, hallways, toilets, overflowing wastebaskets, administrators, coworkers, teachers, students, and at least once, the lunchroom ladies.

His rage and anger knew no apparent boundaries and once extended to our superintendent of schools, Alvin T. Stolen, whom Frank removed from the building. Stolen attended a band concert in the Washington auditorium and after the performance had gone to compliment the band director. His visit extended beyond 10:00 p.m., by which time all visitors were to be out of the school.

As the superintendent was meandering down the third-floor hall, Frank spied him. "Out!" he barked. "It's after ten o'clock. Out." The verbal assault startled Stolen. "Frank," he said, "do you know who I am?"

Frank didn't, but he said, "I don't give a good goddamn who you are. Out. Out, now." He escorted the distinguished gentleman to the Lake Avenue exit, and Stolen turned to his employee and simply said, "You're doing a good job, Frank."

The following day when Frank found out who he'd evicted, his reaction was typically Frank. "I don't care who he is, no sonabitch is in my building after ten o'clock."

His visage reflected a man angry at the world and all its inhabitants. I only once saw him smile. During the winter the school softball field was flooded for use as a skating rink. One winter the school hired an Italian immigrant to tend the rink. Following basketball practice one afternoon, a few of us were crossing the ice—a shortcut to our bus stop. Frank was approaching from the opposite direction and between us was the rink attendant with a broom, shooing a dog of spaniel-collie mix from the premises. As he turned to hail Frank, the canine went for him, but not with his teeth. The attendant yelped and began chasing the animal. "Damn-a dog," he shouted. He piss on-a my leg." We hooted, and even Frank grinned, but it was almost grotesque, so out of character was mirth for him. "Geez, for a second there, I thought Frank's face might break when he smiled," a mate said as we waited for the bus.

More than anything else, he loathed school dances. In his view these were scheduled solely to keep him from completing his tasks in a timely manner, to say nothing of the additional messes left by adolescent dancers. Monitoring and cleaning the boys' restroom on the second floor vexed him most. Dances were in the basement cafeteria, but there were no toilet facilities for boys until the second floor. And junior high school boys, Frank knew, loved to wad wet toilet paper and splat it against the ceiling. They wouldn't flush toilets, their aim at urinals was sporadic, and they were noisy. To maintain a modicum of control, Frank would lock three of the four commode stalls and would blockade with planks and buckets all but two of the urinals.

Then he'd position himself at the top of the second-floor stairwell, seated on a folding chair with a length of one-by-three board across his lap. During band breaks, boys would start up the stairs to the toilet, and upon reaching the first floor, could hear Frank railing against the "sonsabitches" who planned the dances and the "rotten little bastids" who attended them. As we'd near Frank the cursing would momentarily pause as he'd tell us to hurry the hell up, not piss on the floor, and not upset what he'd already cleaned. "No pushing or shoving, goddammit."

Frank's gruff manner didn't keep us from teasing him. When the boys saw their toileting opportunities limited, they would get Frank's goat by shouting something like "Don't pee in the sink, Eddie. Frank'll raise holy hell." That was all he needed and he'd come rushing into the bathroom, one-by-three at the ready. "You guys think you're funny? I give you a crack on the ass, and you won't laugh."

One spring Friday night, when I was in ninth grade and attending the last dance of the year, a friend, Paul, and I climbed the stairs to the boys' room following an intermission. We had learned not to use the toilet while the band was on break but to wait until dancing resumed, when we didn't have to stand in line. As we neared Frank, he shot a glance at us and snarled, "You guys don't come here to dance, you come here to shit."

THOUGH OLD FRANK was the most unforgettable character of my school days, there was also Enoch Maki, another school custodian. During the summer of 1957, Dad arranged for me to work with the crews that cleaned city schools during summer vacation. Each crew paired several temporary workers with a few permanent school employees. The heavier tasks, like scrubbing floors, were assigned to the younger college-age men; the older veterans mostly washed desktops—a relatively simple chore where they could sit on a stool and wipe each desk with a damp sponge. Once in a while, one of the older workers lagged behind, and our foreman, Bob Graves, occasionally ordered a temp worker to a classroom with Enoch, our oldest man, to accelerate completion.

Enoch, in his late sixties, spoke little English, though he apparently understood it well enough to fulfill his responsibilities. One afternoon I learned his English comprehension exceeded what the rest of the crew anticipated.

We had been sent to clean the old West Junior High School. It was near Cody Street, which had been named for William Cody—Buffalo Bill—who had built a house there. Though Cody never lived in the home, his sister occupied it for many years.

While Lloyd Hackl and I were scrubbing the hallway on first floor, Enoch was wiping desktops in a nearby classroom. Lloyd and I started to riff on Buffalo Bill, positing that Cody was a sissy who rode sidesaddle and was a pure huckster who knew little about the real Wild West. Suddenly a livid Enoch emerged in the doorway, a sopping sponge in his clenched fist, which he shook at us. He began raging in Finnish, broken only by the occasional sputtering of "Buffalo Bill" in English. Clearly we had messed with a man Enoch revered as an icon, a hero to Duluthians of Enoch's age. His inflection and arm gestures suggested a desire to choke the life out of both of us.

Thereafter I had little to do with Enoch. He always avoided Lloyd and me on coffee or lunch breaks. Enoch was an inveterate consumer of chewing tobacco, and I never saw him remove a chew even while eating. He did, however, spit often. Other users of smokeless tobacco who worked with us carried pork-and-beans can spittoons; Enoch deposited Copenhagen residues in his left shirt pocket. These pockets were deeply stained and we always pondered what Enoch's wife thought when laundering those shirts with snoose-brown pockets. Enoch preferred work shirts of light blue or tan, so the stains were especially prominent and indelible.

A week and a half after the Buffalo Bill episode, Bob Graves delegated me to help Enoch clean desks at Emerson Elementary School. Lloyd smirked. "Watch it," he whispered to me, and I asked what he meant. "Enoch spits," Lloyd said, "and when he's washing desks, he doesn't spit in his pocket; he uses his water bucket. When he gets a chance he'll spit in your bucket too." Throughout that day I kept one eye on Enoch and the other on my bucket. By lunchtime, his "cleaning water" was thick and brackish from tobacco juice. All morning he washed children's desks without changing water.

Over the years I've often thought of those little kids with shining morning faces, arriving in class and sitting at desks that had literally been spit-polished by Enoch Maki.

IN MY EXPERIENCE there were no Frank- or Enoch-type characters on faculties, but we had a few otherwise pleasant, friendly folks at Denfeld in the early 1960s who displayed unique eccentricities that were ignored or simply attributed to "the way he/she is."

Carl, for instance, used to corner me practically every week, urging me to marry soon and begat children immediately before my seed went bad. Carl had taken care of his widowed mother until her death and did not marry until he was nearly forty-seven. A son was born just before Carl turned fifty, and the boy had some developmental disabilities. "It was all my fault," Carl used to say. "By the time I got married my seed was old, and as every farmer knows, old seed isn't worth a damn."

G. Dell Daedo, our principal at the time, eschewed shaking hands and grimaced each time protocol forced him to grip another's palm. As soon as possible he'd bolt for the faculty lounge to give his hands a thorough scrubbing. He also refused to touch doorknobs and would insert his hand in the pocket of his suit jacket and use the fabric as a barrier between his fingers and the germ-infested knob.

Daedo used to munch ice-cream bars while he patrolled the school cafeteria during lunch periods—except he didn't consume the treat the way everyone else did. Forsaking the stick holding the bar, he'd wrench it free of the ice cream while the bar was in the bag, then crush the chocolate coating with his hands and eat from the bag with a spoon. He also ingested popcorn via spoon, one kernel at a time.

Late in the year our assistant principal became ill and was considering retirement. A fellow teacher who coveted the position soon began following Daedo through the cafeteria aping the boss's ice-cream bar and popcorn-consuming habits. When the assistant principal did retire, guess who was named as replacement?

Then there was the faculty meeting when Daedo asked for new business, and Herb, the school's business manager, rose. He'd been noticing that several campus organizations were leaving sacks of cash—receipts from sales or dues—in the safe at the end of school-days, without indicating either the amount of money or the name of the organization. "If a break-in or burglary should occur, we'd have no accurate records for insurance," Herb said. "So if you're a club adviser please leave a note with your deposit indicating the name of the organization and the amount of cash in the bag."

As Herb sat, a wag from the history department stood. "Herb," he said, smiling, "how do we know the burglar wouldn't snap up those notes too? Then we'd be right back where we started."

"Oh, I don't think he would bother with the notes," Herb said. "He'd just be interested in the money—cash on the barrelhead and get out quick."

"Now hold on a second," someone else piped. "Who's to say that the burglar would be male? Could just as well be a woman, couldn't it?"

That remark piqued several women—the sewing teacher in particular. "Of course it would be a man. You never hear of women sneaking around at night breaking into buildings. Maybe her boyfriend might have her wait in the car or something, but it's ridiculous to think a woman would break into Denfeld High School, smash open a safe, and grab money and notes. That's the dumbest thing I ever heard."

This discourse persisted for more than ten minutes before a perplexed principal suggested the issue be tabled until the next meeting. But it didn't surface then or at any future gathering before the end of the school year, by which time I'd submitted my resignation to attend graduate school at Kent State University in Ohio.

THE VOICE

WHO KNEW THAT IN A WORLD where a boy at Duluth Central High School would persistently beg acquaintances to put him on stage in their skits, and whose first roles were nonspeaking, that boy would a couple of decades later become the most prominent voice-over actor of his generation?

During the school year 1956–57, Ray Karkkainen and I used to script and stage a number of skits for school programs. Many of them were for pep assemblies on days of football or basketball games. Kark and I thought our material witty and smart. So did Don, an underclassman who wanted to hang with us and perform in our pieces. Alas, he was mostly disappointed; we thought he was a nice kid but had not, in our estimation, demonstrated enough talent to secure a role of any significance—until one all-school assembly where Ray and I were asked to produce a few olios in front of the curtain while crews were setting up for the next acts.

We found a part for Don LaFontaine, the kid who pestered us. After blacking his teeth, we gave him two boxes of Chiclets chewing gum, instructing him to put six or eight pieces in his mouth. He was to be menaced by Bobby Cohen, a class comic, who'd feign punching him in the mouth several times as they paraded across the stage in front of the curtain. Following each punch, Don spit out two or three Chiclets, which clattered on the floor. Neither actor spoke, and the bit was repeated three different times during the hour. Following the final routine, Don faced the audience and flashed a broad "toothless" smile.

He loved his first-ever appearance on stage and urged us to cast him again. I put him in another sketch that supported a home-coming queen candidate. Don wore a large sack over his head with eyeholes cut out. No one could tell who he was, and again he had no lines. Whether he appeared in any of Ray's future skits, I can't recall.

KARK AND I GRADUATED from Central and went on to the University of Minnesota–Duluth where we both participated in theater, though he was more active as I drifted into folk music performance. During our college years we lost contact with Don but heard that he utilized what we'd taught him the previous year to do more acting and speaking during his senior year at Central. He was voted wittiest boy by the class of 1958, succeeding Ray, who had earned that distinction the year before. I also learned that Don went into the military after high school, becoming a recording engineer for U.S. Army music ensembles.

In the meantime, after a two-year army stint of his own, Ray went to Hollywood and found sporadic television work with Red Skelton and in sitcoms like *The Andy Griffith Show*. He landed a feature role in Norman Lear's film *Cold Turkey*, but it was TV commercials and print ads where he earned a livelihood. During the early 1980s, Ray called once and said he'd run into Don, who was involved with producing radio promotions for movies, and that Don said to say hi.

Far from the old stage at Duluth Central, LaFontaine was building his own career in show business using his resonant, rich voice in what would be more than five thousand film trailers and pitches for Chevrolets, Fords, Budweiser, McDonald's, Coke products, and many others for more than thirty years until his death in 2008 from a pulmonary embolism.

LaFontaine earned millions relying on that voice, called by Hollywood insiders the "Thunder Throat," and became famous for his signature line: "In a world . . ."

Ray and I cast LaFontaine because he badgered us and because we needed someone who wouldn't refuse a minor, nonspeaking role.

We meant well, but Don's eventual success humbled us. What did we know? How could we not recognize his potential? When I'd heard Don had joined the army, I figured him for an infantry grunt. Sure, in a way we gave him his first experience before audiences, but we didn't utilize his great voice because we weren't impressed.

In a way our minimizing Don's inordinate vocal gift calls to mind the acquaintance who was a member of the fraternity young Bobby Zimmerman was pledging during his freshman year at the University of Minnesota. Zimmerman wasn't social and spent his time plunking on a guitar and growling out unfamiliar songs. "A lot of us thought his music was weird, and we didn't think he sang well either," the fellow said. "I thought he wouldn't get voted in, so one day I told him to engage with us more, stop playing songs nobody could sing along to, and put the guitar away." He paused. "What if he had listened to me?" A lot of frat boys at the University failed to recognize the budding genius who became Bob Dylan.

There are other examples of tyros in many endeavors who were initially dismissed by persons who thought themselves qualified to pronounce judgments on someone's potential. But in a world where promise may go unrecognized and unappreciated for a time, Don LaFontaine, an eager, ambitious kid from Duluth, overcame those early, flawed assessments of his capabilities to become known throughout the film industry as the "Voice of God."

BEWARE THE IDES OF MARCH,
OR THE DEATH OF IAGO

THE IDES OF MARCH just aren't what they used to be. You can't find many folks who beware them anymore. I may be one of the exceptions. My own bewaring began during my sophomore year at the University of Minnesota–Duluth when an adviser suggested I would do well to brush up on my Shakespeare. He enrolled me in the course The Tragedies of William Shakespeare, taught by William Rosenthal, head of the English department.

As chance would have it, an old friend, Ron Raver, was also enrolled, and since he was the only other student I knew in the class, I chose a seat next to him. An established prankster, he had gained a degree of notoriety that fall for grabbing a megaphone at the annual homecoming bonfire and hollering, "Theater! Theater!" When the several hundred attendees looked puzzled but otherwise did not react, Ron concluded that yelling "Theater" at a crowded fire was perfectly legal and did not infringe free speech—a point he later argued in a philosophy class.

A skilled impressionist, Ron blurted "Beware the Ides of March" in a Boris Karloffian voice one Friday following Dr. Rosenthal's announcement that we would begin our analysis of *Julius Caesar* on Monday. The phlegmatic professor was not amused, and he asked Ron to refrain from such outbursts in the future.

Later in the term, Dr. Rosenthal was guiding us through *Othello*. He fell behind in his syllabus schedule, which called for one period to be dedicated to each of the five acts. We were to start with act 1 on Monday and conclude with act 5 on Friday. Monday and Tuesday's sessions stalled on the first act, and act 2 had not been completed at the end of Thursday's class. I saw no need to conclude the reading by Friday either, assuming discussion of *Othello* would continue well into the following week.

So I was surprised on Friday when Dr. Rosenthal hastened through acts 3, 4, and 5, nearly finishing the play. With five minutes remaining in the period, he was philosophizing about how jealousy had corrupted Iago. As the professor filed lecture notes in his briefcase, he looked up. "Mr. Fedo," he said, gazing expectantly in my direction, "what happens to Iago at the end of the fifth act?"

My stomach lurched and rolled. I didn't know. Hearkening to earlier discussions of *Julius Caesar* and *Macbeth* it seemed reasonable to assume that the villainous Iago would have doubtless received the ultimate comeuppance—death at the hands of noble avengers.

After an awkward, uncomfortable pause, I spoke.

"Iago died."

A momentary silence was punctuated by the nervous giggling of several other students.

Ron was on his feet. "Iago died? Iago died?" his voice ascended shrilly, accusing. "Iago didn't die. You didn't finish reading the play, did you? The death of Iago. Now I've heard everything."

During this tirade, Dr. Rosenthal meandered up the aisle to the back of the room where Ron hovered over me. He put his hand on Ron's shoulder, easing him back into his seat and urged him to calm down. As Dr. Rosenthal returned to the lectern the bell sounded, ending class, but the professor held up his hand. "We may assume, Mr. Fedo, that Iago did indeed die, as all humans do. I was, however, referring to his fate at the end of this play."

I had hoped to wrangle a B in the course, but that hope was dashed with the blunder about Iago's demise. Less than two weeks remained in the term and I couldn't imagine how I might reinstate myself in Dr. Rosenthal's esteem.

An opportunity availed itself in the last week of the quarter, when I managed a particularly perspicacious response to another of Dr. Rosenthal's queries, this time concerning *Hamlet*. I postulated before the class that when Hamlet dismisses Ophelia with "Get thee to a nunnery," he might have been referring not to an abbey but rather to a brothel.

This contribution enthralled our professor, who seemed eager to pursue the point. Beaming, he descended on me. "How very intriguing, Mr. Fedo," he exclaimed. I had done it; I had redeemed myself and was prepared to bask in the glow of the teacher's plaudits—until I saw Ron leap up. "Isn't it incredible, Dr. Rosenthal, that this man, who brilliantly expounds on an obscure hypothesis about *Hamlet*, less than two weeks ago tried to convince us that Iago died?"

That day was March 15, and though it happened more than forty years ago, I still flush at the recollection, and I've been bewaring ever since.

One March ides in the mid-1970s, a large pheasant flew into the windshield of my VW beetle, cracking it. Several years later I lost my youngest daughter for nearly an hour in the Minneapolis Dayton's department store. And last year on March 15, a delivery person demolished my computer when it slipped from his hands and disassembled on our driveway.

You'll understand then that when this March 15 rolls around. I'll be a bit jumpy. My wife says I'm being paranoid. Maybe so. But even if that's true, it doesn't mean someone or something isn't out to get me.

HE BELIEVED WRITERS
ARE MADE, NOT BORN

IN THE 1950S, when Ed Krzenski began teaching English, many of his contemporaries had already abandoned the Sisyphean struggle to equip their pupils with writing skills. The notion that writers are born—not made—was gaining credence in faculty lounges across the United States. In place of learning how to write, some teachers were asking students to respond orally to stories, essays, or poems rather than having students analyze the literature in writing, let alone fashion their own poetry or prose.

This didn't sit well with Ed, who believed that writing could be taught and that nearly anyone could be trained to write passably. He was the finest writing teacher I have known, and if his name is unfamiliar to you it's because he labored in obscurity at Cloquet High School in Minnesota teaching eleventh-grade English. I don't think he ever published anything, and he never aspired to. But all of Ed's students learned to write or they didn't pass his class.

He used to say it was a shame that so many English teachers and professors believed that writing was an innate skill that could not be taught. It was a shame because Ed could teach it and teach it well. He certainly did during the spring quarter of 1962 when I was completing my degree at the University of Minnesota–Duluth and practice-teaching under his tutelage.

During those several months, I watched a man dedicate himself to teaching writing to teens whose interests were anywhere but in the schoolroom, where they were required to parse sentences. Ed was the only high school teacher I'm aware of whose students wore out books of grammar.

His raison d'être was ensuring that every high school junior enrolled in his class would leave understanding what constituted a sentence, a paragraph, and an essay and knowing how to execute them.

"I stress writing," he informed me the day I arrived in Cloquet. His comment was pointed; my background was literature, and I had expected to emphasize that during my apprenticeship. "The trend these days is away from writing and grammatical rules, but I'm from the old school."

Except he wasn't that old—late thirties perhaps; he was of medium height and build and wore dark horn-rimmed glasses with lenses that magnified his eyes.

"Kids can learn how to write," he said, "and the ones in my classes will learn."

Ed insisted that every pupil could write solid exposition—essays and criticism—after proper instruction. His directions demanded that students pore over grammar workbooks, complete the exercises, and pay scrupulous attention to numerous discussions about developing and supporting a thesis.

His students wrote a five-hundred-word theme each week, which meant Ed was reading about one hundred papers per week—a total of more than fifty thousand words. He demanded quality submissions, complete with proper usage, grammatical perfection, and correct spelling. Students were required to demonstrate comprehension of each week's ten vocabulary words by using them in their essays.

Ed meticulously examined each paper but would not record a grade until it was error-free, an often maddening process for the students. At the top of a returned theme, Ed noted the types of errors in the paper, such as spelling, awkward construction, or grammar. But the notes would never disclose where the problems were located on the page. The student had to figure that out for him- or herself.

A day or two later Ed would receive the "corrected" paper, sometimes to discover the student had misspelled a second word while missing the original. Now Ed's notation indicated two words were spelled incorrectly. This exchange might go on for days, even weeks, with the paper dishrag-limp from erasures. But before Ed would issue a grade, the entire paper would need to be clear of mistakes.

His approach to discipline also involved writing and words. Instead of detention for fractious or recalcitrant students, Ed insisted they copy, verbatim, everything on an assigned page from a Merriam-Webster dictionary, including the diacritical marks. During the time I spent observing and teaching his classes, I learned that even the students he labeled as average possessed working vocabularies far exceeding those of most of my college peers.

By the end of Ed's second-hour class each day, perspiration glistened behind his glasses, and his shirt was damp—the result of his ceaseless efforts to instill a belief among his students that using words and writing well has utilitarian value far beyond the classroom.

In the more than forty years since I left Cloquet High School, I have published eight books and a batch of stories and essays in respectable journals and newspapers. Yet I'm sure nothing I've written has carried the power and impact of Ed's teaching.

His students learned how a stronger command of the English language can better prepare them for tackling complex issues—a skill that demands clarity of thought and expression. There can be little doubt that when acuity of language is diminished, we are more easily flummoxed by politicians, advertisers, and talk-radio hosts. Our own thoughts are reduced to nods, shrugs, and an irritating plethora of "you know."

"Most people don't realize that writing well teaches you to think clearly," Ed told me one warm afternoon as that long-ago spring term wound down. "The world may not need more authors, but sadly, there will always be a shortage of clear thinkers."

So whenever the idea that writing can't be taught surfaces at writers' workshops and conferences where I am a participant, I always hearken back to Ed Krzenski's comment about those who teach writing but believe it can't be taught. "If someone really believes that, he should have the integrity to not cash his paycheck."

SINCLAIR LEWIS'S DULUTH

IN 1970, A TRAVEL EDITOR at the *Los Angeles Times* asked me to go to Sauk Centre, Minnesota, Sinclair Lewis's boyhood home, and write an article about the town believed to be the model for Gopher Prairie in the novel *Main Street*. *Main Street* was first published in 1920, and my piece would tie in with the fiftieth anniversary of the book's release.

Ben Dubois was the last person alive in Sauk Centre who was born the same year as Lewis—1885—and who grew up with him. He affirmed that life in Sauk Centre was often painful for Harry Sinclair Lewis, though in a letter Lewis wrote to a graduating class at his old high school he said it was a good place in which to grow up. Yet Lewis keenly felt a measure of displacement in this small community; he was a runty kid with a bad complexion who couldn't earn the affection of his physician father and felt inferior to his older brother, Claude, who would follow their father into medicine.

Dubois was eighty-five when I met him at his desk in the lobby of the Sauk Centre Bank. He had been retired for years but still held court there greeting area residents, mainly old farmers or their descendants who accorded him respect bordering on reverence. During the Depression, Dubois kept his bank open, never foreclosed on a delinquent farmer, and suffered along with nearly every other resident of Stearns County. It was with some pride he told me, soon after we had shaken hands, that he'd once cast a presidential vote for the socialist Eugene Debs.

Dubois was a raconteur, full of stories about his old boyhood chum. "Harry was a homely, ornery chap," he recalled. "Nobody liked him very much, which made him the butt of practical jokes. One time he wanted to tag along with some older boys, and because he was a sucker for pranks, they let him. They said they were going to gather hazelnuts. Well, they scooped up a couple of handfuls of rabbit droppings, told Harry they were hazelnuts, and got him to eat a good share of them before he figured things out.

"He didn't do particularly well in school either, which displeased his father. To tell the truth, nobody around here ever thought he'd amount to very much. He was never happy here, but then he wasn't happy anyplace else either, was he?"

I asked Dubois if he knew anything about Lewis's Duluth residency.

"Well, now, I don't think he liked it at all, but, you see, he was there to do some research. He captured the city rather well, don't you think? It's all there in *Babbitt* and *Kingsblood Royal*. Pretty much captured it, if you ask me."

AT A GENERAL CONFERENCE Baptist convention in Duluth one 1940s summer, our pastor, Marvin Samuelson, spied Sinclair Lewis in attendance taking copious notes during presentations. Fearing that Lewis's observations might later find their way into another novel even more spurious than *Elmer Gantry*, our pastor made so bold as to approach the noted cynic to inquire after the condition of his soul and might he wish spiritual counseling?

Lewis spurned the offer but was quite civil during the exchange, which lasted several minutes. He even thanked Reverend Samuelson, when our minister said he'd pray for Lewis anyway.

After learning of this encounter—offhandedly inserted into one of the preacher's Sunday sermons—Mother mentioned she'd been loaned a copy of *Elmer Gantry* some years before and found it so loathsome that she'd thrown the book, which didn't belong to her, in the furnace.

I checked out the novel at the library during my sophomore year in high school, and unlike Mother, found it troubling rather than disgusting. I didn't see Reverend Samuelson in the Elmer Gantry character, but I thought it possible that there were Gantrys sermonizing elsewhere in America.

Following *Elmer Gantry,* I checked out another Lewis novel, *Kingsblood Royal,* after learning he'd written it while living in Duluth.

ADRIFT AFTER HIS DIVORCE from Dorothy Thompson in 1942, Lewis moved to Duluth during the winter of 1944 and settled into an expansive house in the east end of town that he described as "[Duluth's] best residential section." He rented and then purchased the home at 2601 East Second Street and was assigned the phone number of Hemlock 6817. "It is a kind of manor home," he wrote in a letter to his paramour, Marcella Powers. "Brick, enter a little court-yard, big drawing room, paneled library, furniture rather shabby, but most comfortable, 5 masters bedrooms with 3 baths, a couple servants rooms, in the basement a jolly foolish miniature bowling alley and a game room. . . . I think I shall love my manorial splendor."

He was captivated by the physical attractiveness of our city on a hill overlooking Lake Superior, and in another letter to Powers he wrote, "Duluth is as individual and beautiful as ever—more magic than when I last saw it now that [the] Skyline Parkway [is] completed." Lewis loved looking down on Duluth and the harbor from that new roadway atop the city, stretching practically its entire length.

An entry from his diary on Tuesday, May 11, 1944, reads: "It's amazing how much happier I am here than in Hollywood a year ago, with all its Kate Hepburns and Cedrick Hardwickes and Romanoff Restaurants." But he also wrote to Powers, "I have found the people here kind, friendly, and about as ponderously dull . . . as any I have ever known outside the pages of that gt masterpiece 'Babbitt.'" About the Duluth men who joined the Chamber of Commerce, he wrote, "They are peculiar to America and in 'Babbitt' I just began to paint them."

In Duluth, too, his awareness of racism was heightened and would be central to *Kingsblood Royal.* The main character, Neil Kingsblood, discovers he is one-thirty-second black and encounters unexpected northern Minnesota racists. While reading it, I recalled a comment Mother had made when I was nine years old about the

1920 lynching of three Negroes in town that took place less than a mile and a half from our house.

Lewis would have known about these lynchings since reports of a ten-thousand-person mob storming the local jail generated national news and also because while he lived in Duluth one of his friends was Kenneth Cant, son of Judge William Cant, who convened the grand jury to consider indictments following the hangings. Some Duluth acquaintances speculated that it was the lynchings that impelled him to write Neil Kingsblood's story.

Increasingly conscious of racism in American society, Lewis sometimes expressed ambivalence about employing black domestics to succor him in his baronial estate. But he occasionally accompanied those same servants to services at St. Mark African Methodist Episcopal Church at 502 East Sixth Street where he witnessed black citizens worshipping and conversing as he gathered material for *Kingsblood Royal,* a novel that would influence the writing of my own first book in 1978. Spurred by Lewis's analysis of racism in my county, I chronicled the June 15, 1920, murders in *The Lynchings in Duluth.*

Prior to the appearance of *Kingsblood Royal* in 1947, Lewis wrote another novel at his Duluth domicile—*Cass Timberlane*—which was published two years earlier. His courtship of Marcella Powers, an actress thirty-five years his junior, framed the setting that explored aspects of a May–December relationship in this novel.

MY HOMETOWN WAS ABUZZ with excitement in the fall of 1968 after a CBS television producer picked the city to be featured in a documentary called *The Great American Novel.* Sinclair Lewis's *Babbitt* was to be featured in the program, and Duluth was thought to be the setting for the fictional Zenith in the book, probably because of our town's sobriquet: the Zenith City of the unsalted seas. Though Lewis himself once said Chicago was his model for Zenith, the disclaimer was never taken seriously, probably owing to Lewis's Duluth residency.

The producer secured cooperation from Duluth's commercial and civic establishments for the project that was slated for telecast the following spring. The actor Pat Hingle was hired to narrate the script, and shooting commenced.

The local Lions Club, delighted that the entire country would see the town celebrated on national television, hosted a luncheon for the cast and crew at the conclusion of the filming, which the producer suggested might be included in the broadcast. Prominent citizens snapped up tickets, ignoring the superintendent of schools, Laverne Rasmussen, who warned that they were about to be bamboozled, that Babbitt was not a complimentary figure nor was Zenith a beacon of enlightenment. He urged them to read the novel because the program might reveal that Babbittry in the city was unchanged from the time Lewis published the book.

During the fete, there were speeches by community leaders before the program producer announced that Hingle would like to treat the audience to a few paragraphs from the novel. He delivered word for word the chauvinistic succeed-in-business-platitudes and condemnation-of-liberal-intellectuals declamation given by George Babbitt in the book to the Zenith Real Estate Board. The Lions, however, seemed to have missed the point that this was Babbitt's speech, and they frequently interrupted a startled and bemused Hingle with thunderous applause. When he finished, Hingle was accorded a standing ovation. Naturally the segment was incorporated into the telecast. Despite his satirical renown, Lewis rarely laughed, but he certainly would have enjoyed seeing the parallels between Duluth and his Zenith on national television.

DESPITE LEWIS'S DISPARAGING TAKE on those who aspired to wealth and prominence, in Duluth his associates included judges, business and civic leaders, as well as the socialite–novelist Margaret Culkin Banning. A casual assessment of Lewis's term in Duluth might conclude that he was relatively happy and successful. But happiness wasn't in the cards for the winner of the 1930 Nobel Prize for Literature. Invited to give the 1945 commencement speech at Duluth State Teachers' College (now the University of Minnesota–Duluth), he delivered an address titled "The Excitement of Learning" and told friends he was disappointed in what he called an ungracious reception. Even so, he later lectured on the craft of writing to students in English classes.

Some entries in his Minnesota diaries touch on his pleasure with the city's scenic beauty and his enjoyment of concerts given by the Duluth Symphony Orchestra under the direction of Tauno Hannikainen, whom he knew socially.

But Lewis's sojourn in Duluth was relatively brief—less than two years. His research on the region completed, he moved on. Always a solitary figure, Lewis was alone when he died in a Rome hospital in 1951.

"His funeral was here in Sauk Centre," said Ben Dubois. "Lots of literary folk stop by the cemetery to pay their respects. Seems sad in a way that more people visit his grave than visited him while he was alive. Not that Harry was that high on social affairs and small talk." Suffused with alcohol, Lewis made caustic and belittling remarks to well-meaning people whose intellect he deemed inferior to his.

Though his insults soured the atmosphere at social gatherings, he nonetheless seemed to crave discourse while in Duluth, as he did throughout his life. Margaret Culkin Banning went out of her way to introduce him to residents who were pleased to entertain so eminent a celebrity. While often appearing to enjoy their company, Lewis could not help observing them with his writerly eye, and as he did with his hometown gentry, he could not resist illumining their foibles in his fiction.

DINERS, DIVES, NO DRIVE-INS

DURING MY HIGH SCHOOL and college years in Duluth, the land-mark Joe Huie's Café on Lake Avenue below Superior Street figured prominently in the social lives of my penurious peers. There was a sign in front that read: LOST KEY WE NEVER CLOSE. Joe Huie's was open 24/7. The restaurant featured Cantonese fare, and servings were both bounteous and cheap. A bowl of chop suey cost 90 cents and so did a platter of egg foo young. On a student budget, one could achieve gustatory satiation at Joe's.

Joe Huie's late-night gathering was motley: drifters, down-at-the-heels men with stubble beards and ripped denims (decades before fashionable), the occasional over-the-hill lady of the evening, cleaning women, night janitors, street preachers, pool sharks, gamblers, cops, and sartorially elegant executives mingled with colorful residents of the adjacent Metropole Hotel. A number of Metropole men were eccentrics who sometimes provided amusement. I recall one incident when two Metropolians, deep in their cups, were sitting at the counter spooning food mouthward—not always success-fully—and arguing about whether the chicken in their dishes was really chicken. One of them said it was pigeon that Joe caught on the street. He said he didn't mind pigeon; he ate them at home all the time during the Depression. Finally, the other man said he'd call a waitress for the truth. Whereupon his mate dumped a glass of water into the other's lap, sending the fellow scurrying upstairs for a change of clothes. During his absence both plates were polished off.

There was a bar on the Metropole's ground floor, and if you desired a libation to accompany an item from Huie's, you sat in a rear booth at the Met and summoned a waitress from next door who'd come through the connecting hallway to take your order.

Joe's longtime waitresses were mostly women of perpetual middle age who kept their brown or bleached-blond hair in buns and greeted customers wearing world-weary countenances. They spent decades observing the human strata in Duluth but were not impressed with status; the mayor or the bowery habitué was greeted with "Hi, there. Know what ya want?" You'd likely be recognized after several visits, and if you left tips, you were sometimes slipped an extra egg roll or almond cookie.

During my college days, when one of our crowd was interested in a particular coed, we'd always inquire, "Do you think you can take her to Joe's?" If the young lady not only agreed but also ordered something beyond a Coke, you knew this gal was worth pursuing.

More often, however, my pals and I met at the café after we'd dropped off our dates, because in those days female residents of dormitories had a 1:00 a.m. curfew on weekends. We'd tease and cajole waitresses: "Hey, who's the best-looking guy here? Tip you a buck if you get it right." Or we'd engage regulars in disparate discourses about boxing, politics, or the local television celebrity, three sheets to the wind at the end of the counter.

One night when a friend and I stopped in shortly after 1:00 a.m., we sat at the counter next to a man who looked like a regular from the West Superior Street bowery. Unkempt and unshaven, absent of upper and lower incisors, he was redolent of some cheap vino du jour. He figured us as college boys, saying with our education we must know "an awful lot of crap," and he asked us what we thought about clouds.

"What do you mean, what do we think about clouds?" my friend said. "Clouds are clouds like nimbostratus or cumulus. What's to think about?"

The old guy cackled. "Young man, clouds are where angels hide out. You don't believe me? You and a million others. College boys." He grunted. "There's things not in books, you know. Now you boys consider this: when you get a heavy fog, which is nothin' but low clouds, you got angels hiding inside to get close for a good look at things down here." He paused, sipped tea, and said, "I never been to college, only got far as eighth grade, but I got things up here," he said, tapping his temple with a bony forefinger, "that nobody else ever thought of. One day, I'm gonna write a book." He probed the suey with his fork, emerging with a small piece of rubber tubing. "What the hell is this?" he said.

"A bamboo shoot?" my friend offered.

He grunted, jabbed the fork into his mouth and vigorously masticated the foreign object. Finally he spat. "Bastard," he growled. "It's rubber tubing."

I held a finger to my lips. "Shh. You got the only one."

Another Joe Huie incident stands out, occurring on the very last day of the restaurant's existence. I was in Duluth with my wife Judy and baby daughter, Kimberly, visiting my parents. Hungry for Chinese I suggested phoning Huie's for takeout.

A woman answered, and after listening to our seven-item order, said, "Sir, I can't talk now, because we're on fire."

I assumed there was some minor conflagration on the stove, and I could call back in a few minutes. The return call went unanswered. Not a minor kerfuffle at all; that fire temporarily shut down Joe Huie's.

THOUGH A BEER COST only 15 cents at the Metropole next to Huie's, the darkened interior held more appeal for older serious imbibers, so after concerts, convocations, or the theater, my pals and I adjourned to the Pickwick at 508 East Superior Street. The Pickwick had the ambience of a German *Brauhaus*—heavy, dark wood furnishings, the walls festooned with mounted fish and game. A stein of locally brewed Fitger's beer was a quarter, and as I recall, a Polish sausage sandwich cost less than two bucks.

The Pickwick staff, however, was not pleased to see college boys come through the door. Students rarely tipped, or if they did they left only the nickel and dime change that had been returned by the server. Judging from the pinched countenances of the waitresses approaching our table, we sensed they had drawn the short straw. There was one exception: Eleanor. At first her sour demeanor resembled that of the others, and her voice was a cigarette-raspy growl. "What the hell ya want?" she said at our initial encounter. I ordered a stein and a Polish sausage. My friend Ron Raver said, "I'll have the same thing except instead of the beer bring me a bourbon and water, and instead of the Polish, I'll have onion rings." Eleanor's frowning face broke into a smile, and she laughed.

Eleanor looked and sounded older than her forty-something years due to her creased face, graying hair, and scratchy voice. After that first meeting, whenever we went to the Pickwick Eleanor always headed to our table, where in exchange for a song of our own composing, she'd buy us a round of beer, or our spontaneous poems about her or her bosses might lead her to let us run a food tab on her account to be paid when convenient. Her generosity was manifest on those occasions when we'd enter and in Ron's words find ourselves "financially embarrassed."

"Well, write me something." Eleanor would say. We titled one "Quatrains on Three Napkins"—it was doggerel, but she laughed long and hard. Her favorite, penned by Ron, was "Ode to Eleanor," ending with these lines: Eleanor, Eleanor/ Flower of the Phlegethon/ Clasp me to your bosom/ I'm cold."

Eleanor was no student of mythology, but the verse delighted her. She committed it to memory and recited the piece on several occasions.

On slow nights Eleanor might pull up a chair and join us for a few moments, during which she talked about her children. "My seven-year-old said the cutest thing last night. My husband told him he had to put his toys away, and he didn't want to. I heard him muttering while he worked, and when I got close I heard him saying over and over, 'Son of a bitch. Son of a bitch.' Seven years old . . . Wonder where he learned that?" She chuckled. "He's the cutest little guy."

Several years after leaving Duluth for graduate school, I returned for a visit. I asked about Eleanor, whom I didn't see. A young waitress said she didn't know Eleanor, but an older employee might remember her.

A few moments later a woman came to my table with the unhappy news that Eleanor had died more than a year ago. "I don't think she was even fifty," the woman said.

I hoisted a glass to our friend.

WHILE IN HIGH SCHOOL I pulled an occasional weekend shift at Nick's Hamburgers on Superior Street at the western end of Duluth. My good friend Peter Patronas, whose Greek family owned the tiny facility, recruited me for the job. A Central High School football teammate, Peter's journey from Greece to America was unique. When World War II broke out, the Patronases were visiting. They were unable to return to the United States until after the Axis surrender. Peter, a small child at the time, boarded a ship with his parents and siblings, and because of his size, he was returned stateside for the cost of cheap parcel post rather than the price of steerage.

Nick's restaurant resembled a converted streetcar. There were only four counter stools plus a takeout window. The menu was limited to burgers, hot dogs, and chili. There were no cheeseburgers, because the hamburgers were first fried on a stove in the basement (where only one person might comfortably stand), then placed in a vat of sauce, which was chili without beans. Hot dogs were also served with the sauce.

I was instructed to put a handful of salt on the coffee grounds before brewing it in the large urn. It didn't seem to alter the taste at all, though now and then older, longtime customers wondered why the restaurant no longer added egg to the coffee.

Most of my working hours were Saturday nights, when the place would hum after neighborhood bars closed at 1:00 a.m. Nick's remained open until about 2:30. During the ninety minutes between bar closings and lights out at Nick's, one encountered a colorful cross-section of humanity, many of whom were in various stages of intoxication.

But I encountered no belligerent drunks; they were mostly in good humor, trading ribald quips back and forth, chiding when someone made off-color comments "in the presence of a lady."

One spring evening, while washing dishes, I detected a small scratching sound in the corner where the hamburger vat had been. A mouse was snacking on spilled crumbs and chili sauce. I grabbed an empty Coke bottle and tossed it in the direction of the rodent. To my surprise (to say nothing of his), the bottle felled the critter. Rather than putting the mouse in the garbage, the prankster in me emerged, and I placed it on a hamburger bun, layering it with catsup and mustard, and topped it with pickles before covering it with the other half of the bun. I took it home wrapped in wax paper.

Monday morning at Central High School, the locker mate of Gordy Ostrov opened Gordy's locker for me, and I placed the mouse-burger in his lunch sack. Gordy was notorious for a squeamish stomach. Even a casual mention by someone ill-prepared for a test that "I think I might throw up" could send our friend rushing from the table.

I was confident Gordy would recognize the wrapped bun as unusual and examine the contents before taking a bite.

Gordy's locker partner had informed others in our lunch group to anticipate a surprise for Gordy, so our table grew silent as he settled himself on a stool and opened the sack. There was a quizzical pause as he viewed the bun and removed the top half; he stared, blanched, and bolted for the bathroom. Two upperclassmen picked up the bun, crossed the divide separating where boys and girls ate, and took the condiment-covered mouse on a tour of the female section, causing great pandemonium among the girls who shrieked or wept and dashed out of the cafeteria. The malefactors were suspended for three days, never knowing (until now) that the entire affair was, in today's argot, my bad.

THOU SHALT NOT SHINE

AT A RECENT REUNION for 1950s and 1960s graduates of the old Duluth Central High School, a woman asked me to sign a book I'd published several years earlier. "It's wonderful that you've written books," she said. "I mean, when we were in school, no one considered that any of us might be authors or physicists or do anything important. I always got the impression we were expected to be average."

The comment of this woman, now a retired professor living in Texas, buttressed my conviction that our hometown was a city with an inferiority complex. Subservience infused our culture. It wasn't precisely articulated; rather, we simply tolerated the jokes about our vile winters and grew quietly petulant with outsiders who let us know they thought we lived in a boondock environment.

I have known other midwesterners who have similar views on where they grew up. Were Des Moines, Omaha, or Madison more provincial than Duluth? Did New Yorkers and Bostonians regard those towns as gulags? What made Duluth stand out, it seemed, was that it had been a target of persiflage for such a very long time.

As far back as 1871, a Kentucky congressman named J. Proctor Knott delivered a speech on the House floor about connecting Duluth to a national railway system, though no one was quite sure where the town was located. Elongating the vowels, he pronounced its name *Duu-loooth*. Many scholars have proclaimed this address the funniest ever delivered in Congress.

Worse, it seems northern Minnesota natives did not catch the satirical drift of Knott's address and later named a Duluth suburb "Proctor" in his honor.

Then there was the Ogden Nash limerick: In Duluth there's a hostess forsooth / Who doesn't know gin from vermouth. / But this lubricant lapse / Isn't noticed perhaps / Because nobody does in Duluth.

WHEN I WAS A STUDENT at the University of Minnesota–Duluth, a folk trio called the Limeliters performed on campus. Between numbers, the group's leader asked, "What do people from Duluth call themselves? Duluthanoids?"

We laughed, of course, but felt the sting of the old stereotype. If you repeat something often enough, it becomes received wisdom. My friends and I grew to believe Duluth deserved its reputation. Nail-in-the-coffin evidence: despite being Minnesota's third-largest city back in the day, Duluth had produced no governors, no U.S. senators, no figure of international renown. (Although Bob Dylan was born here, he was raised in Hibbing.)

We acquiesced to outsiders' perceptions and became a people with limited visions and dreams for our lives. Humility was our chief virtue. "Don't get too big for your britches," was a bromide I heard often while growing up. My generation was instructed to be modest because, as our high school drama coach was fond of saying, we had a lot to be modest about.

In high school we were counseled toward safe career choices. Our teachers, products of the Great Depression, believed the vicissitudes of life were challenge enough; we didn't need equivocation in our employment. Thoughts of making our marks in show business, politics, or professional sports—or finding success in far-off New York, Hollywood, London, or Rome—were daydreams. Reality dictated we would become laborers, teachers, nurses, and clerks, much as our parents before us. Growing up in fear of the world at large-— the world outside Duluth—most of my friends and I hoped to find occupations locally, reducing the threat of finding ourselves adrift, absent of the familiar.

Near the end of my senior year at Central, I had the opportunity to apply for a scholarship at Northwestern University's Medill School of Journalism. I was hesitant; I wouldn't know anyone in Evanston. But the publisher of the *Duluth News Tribune*—himself a Medill graduate—had seen some of my pieces on the Friday teen pages of the newspaper and offered to write a recommendation for me. I declined, with relief, after my father informed me that the starting salary for reporters at the Duluth paper was only $35 per week. It never occurred to me or anyone else that I might work for newspapers in Minneapolis or Chicago. And though the adviser to the school paper believed I had the potential to succeed in journalism, she joined me in deferring to my father's wisdom, and the matter was dropped.

Even if Dad thought I had the talent to work some day for the *New York Times* or CBS, he still might have discouraged this career choice. In his view, those who achieved that kind of prominence were probably full of themselves—big shots who disparaged ordinary people of humble origins. Dad, a second-generation Calabrese, was a Duluth native and a teacher's union officer who had battled local power brokers for fair wages. "Republicans," he used to growl, "eat high off the hog and don't give a damn if anybody else has a slice of bread."

Yet my father never truly tested himself either. A splendid French horn player, Dad was a charter member of the Duluth Symphony Orchestra but refused opportunities to audition for the Minneapolis Symphony Orchestra. "You move to a big city, you just get swallowed up," he would say, and I believed him.

I knew I didn't belong in a major city because a relative who lived in New York knew a rube when she saw one. "You guys dress like you just fell off the turnip truck," she chided us teenage boys during a visit. "Nobody wears white socks if he wants to get on in this world." I did want to get on, but all my friends wore white socks, and I didn't want to be different either.

We lived in the Central Hillside section of town, where most of our Scandinavian and German neighbors—Wally Hassinger, a railroad brakeman; Grant Rowe, an auto mechanic; Hjalmer Haglund, a janitor—often railed against big shots. Everyone lived in plain two-story houses. We grew carrots, tomatoes, lettuce, and beans in backyard gardens, and each Monday the women hung laundry out to dry.

The big shots owned sprawling estates on the east end of town. Descendants of nineteenth-century mining and lumber barons, they were served evening cocktails by domestics. They took steamers to Europe and wintered in Florida or the Bahamas, while hired help cleared snow from their undulating driveways. During spring and summer, gardeners tended their beds of tulips, peonies, and roses. There were neither laundry lines nor vegetable plots in their backyards.

Dad disparaged the prominent for their winter excursions and cringed every time he heard the apocryphal Mark Twain quip, "The coldest winter I ever spent was a summer in Duluth." Leaving town to escape the snow and cold, Dad maintained, bespoke a fragility of character.

There were Duluthians who achieved distinction after leaving the city, but few locals were impressed. The famous curmudgeon Henry Morgan got his start as an announcer at a local radio station, WEBC, before launching his own network show. He became familiar to millions of Americans as a panelist on *What's My Line?* Years earlier, Dorothy Arnold, born in Duluth, went on to Hollywood and appeared in several minor films before becoming Joe DiMaggio's first wife.

Duluth also produced a notable song lyricist named Sammy Gallop, who contributed the words to scores of popular tunes during the 1940s and 1950s, including "Elmer's Tune," "Shoofly Pie and Apple Pan Dowdy," and "Wake the Town and Tell the People." Gallop graduated from Duluth Central in the 1930s, and older teachers who were still around in my day remembered him as a kid who'd wasted his time in the music room, plunking on the piano and filling notebooks with doggerel.

Like Sammy Gallop, some of my peers aspired to vocations beyond Duluth's borders, urging me to move away as well. "If you want to write you should head for New York," said my friend Ray Karkkainen. New York? I'd get swallowed up. But the year after Ray headed for Hollywood, hoping for stardom, I went too—to Kent, Ohio, and graduate school.

Before his untimely death at age forty-nine, Ray managed to carve out a modest career there—mostly in television commercials, but he occasionally landed roles in Norman Lear productions or with Andy Griffith or Red Skelton. He once told me that his Duluth relatives were uncomfortable conversing with him during his visits home.

In their eyes he had become a movie star, and having no experience with celebrities they were reluctant to address the scrawny kid who had been raised among them. Ray's family and boyhood pals couldn't reconcile his nominal fame with their mutual underclass roots.

But other natives were at least mildly impressed by achievements of our fellows. At that 1950s and 1960s class reunion, I heard gossip about the former classmate who became an attorney in the entertainment industry and purchased Liberace's old mansion. Somebody brought up Jerry Music, who went to California, became Lorenzo Music, won Emmys as a writer and performer on the *Smothers Brothers Show*, then created *The Bob Newhart Show* and became even better known as the voice of Garfield in the animated cartoon. They spoke in reverential tones about another boy who became a NASA physicist and also about Don LaFontaine, the narrator for nearly all Hollywood film trailers.

Before returning to Texas, the retired professor sent me a note about the difficulty she'd had in leaving Duluth, first for college, then for a career. She said she experienced an inexorable urge to remain home, to carve a life alongside family and friends in familiar environs. "In the end, I'm glad some of us had the gumption to go," she wrote.

Still, those of us no longer living in Duluth have found ourselves separated from the hometown culture of Scandinavians and Germans for whom stoicism was venerated. Garrison Keillor has it about right: Minnesotans have settled for above average, and we don't blow our own horns. Our ideal world would have no horns for anyone else to blow either. "Do not call attention to thyself" is our eleventh commandment.

I periodically visit relatives in Duluth, though I haven't lived there since the early 1960s. The population, once more than 100,000, has declined by about 15,000. But the once-deteriorating warehouse district on the Lake Superior waterfront now houses tony wine bars, restaurants, and art galleries—a far cry from *New Yorker* writer Philip Hamburger's assessment in a 1950s profile of the city: "Bears love Duluth," he wrote, then went on to explore why our town— with its steep igneous rock hills and Siberian winters—was more hospitable to bruins than humans.

To locals though, the hills, like the winters, have character-building qualities. And surviving subzero blasts and Alberta clipper blizzards are sources of satisfaction. So those who were raised in Duluth but left to find success are not envied. We are pitied in a way, having surrendered to the ease of avoiding slopes and the elements.

"You won't find many pansies here," my father used to say. And he didn't mean flowers.

DAD'S LEGACY

BY ALL ACCOUNTS our father was an admirable man—decent, honest, trustworthy. I omit patience here, because he wasn't patient, and it exacerbated friction between Dad and us boys. The problem, I think, stemmed from the fact that in most human pursuits, he was more adept than his sons.

While David and I excelled in athletics, we didn't equal his achievements. He starred in football and track, where he placed third in the 110-meter low hurdles at the 1929 Minnesota high school track meet, losing to Biggie Munn, later a legendary football coach at Michigan State University. Dad received scholarship offers from major colleges, but turned them down to help support his Depression-era, eleven-person Italian family.

Following his graduation from Denfeld High School, he landed a job with the Oliver Mining Company, painting employees' houses. He was laid off as the Depression deepened, and it occurred to him that attending college was possible. Tuition and fees at Duluth State Teacher's College—now the University of Minnesota–Duluth—were only $2.50 per quarter, which included textbooks. It wasn't the extraordinarily low cost of college back then but the fact that Dad knew how to cut hair, hence he could have a job while in school and continue to aid in supporting the family. Carrying clippers and scissors in a worn leather satchel to class each day, he cut students' and professors' hair for 25 cents in the basement of Torrence Hall on the campus. In the process Dad discovered that teachers survived the Depression with few layoffs, and he determined that kind of job security was for him. Seven years and countless haircuts later, he had his teaching degree.

He routinely led the World War II–era Lakeside Softball League in homeruns. He was physically more powerful than any of his sons, and it galled him when we couldn't heft logs to help him construct our cabin on Island Lake, especially when he could hoist one on his shoulder and climb the escarpment from the lake where he'd floated the logs to the lot on which the cabin would sit. David and I could barely manage getting one log up the hill working together.

Unlike any of the three of us, Dad was a jack-of-all-trades and -arts. An excellent musician, as a charter member of the Duluth Symphony Orchestra he sat in its French horn section for more than thirty years. He could play almost any musical instrument, even cajoling tunes out of the willow whistles he crafted for us when we were kids. Dad made handsome wood furniture and was a professional wood carver, specializing in human forms—loggers, bindle stiffs, fishermen, Santa Claus and elves, and crèches. He taught woodworking in Duluth schools for nearly forty years and wood carving for adults after he retired.

Additionally, he could revive dead mechanical apparatuses, a laudable talent in most circumstances, but at least once it wrought considerable frustration for David and me.

Since we lived next door to our maternal grandmother, David and I were responsible for mowing not only our lawn but Grandma's as well with a manual rotary mower. One day Dad discovered an abandoned gas-powered lawn mower on a scrap heap at the end of Woodland Avenue. He thought if he fooled around with it, he'd get it to run. Succeeding, he gave our reliable old mower away.

He brought David and me to the garage and pointed to the rusty bucket of bolts, as we came to call it. "Isn't new, but she works," he announced. "No more excuses for not mowing." He pulled the starter cord and the machine momentarily sputtered before chugging smoothly. Dad made a couple of passes in our yard before handing it off to me with instructions to finish and take care of Grandma's yard too before supper.

While it was a gas-powered engine, only the blades were affected. There was no drive train, so we still had to manually manipulate the mower, which was considerably heavier than our former clipper. It now required ten to fifteen minutes longer to complete the lawns while concomitantly exhausting the users.

Moreover, the damnable mower would never start for David or me. Each of us would tug the starter rope over and over and over until exhaustion and throbbing shoulders did us in. The infernal machine never even produced an encouraging sputter, let alone fire up and continue.

Each Wednesday, as Dad departed for his summer house-painting labors, he ordered the grass to be cut by the time he returned. Our grumbling that we couldn't start the evil engine only made him furious, so we abandoned the practice and wore out our shoulder muscles until Dad came home, livid upon observing untrimmed yards. Dismissing protests that the mower refused to start, he'd march into the garage and glare. To this day I'm convinced that mower was afraid of Dad and would quiver and snap to attention in his presence. It never failed to start when he administered just ONE pull on the cord. When this happened Dad would look with disgust at David and me and turn his palms upward as if asking God why he was burdened with boys who couldn't start a perfectly good mower. He refused to heed our excuses and complaints.

Actually, he didn't want to hear complaints about anything from his sons, and in particular would not tolerate any mealtime mention of not liking whatever comestibles were placed before us.

To be fair, the no-complaining dictum also applied to him, though persistent sinusitis nullified his sense of taste for many years. One of his "treats" was dried olives saturated with olive oil and hot pepper flakes. He chewed them rapidly like popcorn while watching television. Years later, when the sinus condition improved, he discovered he no longer enjoyed them and would sometimes wrinkle his nose at other viands he had formerly liked.

He'd often go through the refrigerator and remove containers of leftovers, raging that some had become inedible but insisting those that hadn't spoiled be ingested. To that end, he'd combine wieners, baked beans, peas, meatloaf, casseroles, even coleslaw into "omelets" and expect the rest of us to eat them. This practice ended at the same time that the olives ceased appearing. But this was long after the Fedo boys grew to adulthood.

On Mother's behalf, however, she was a fine cook, and there were seldom causes for annoyance regarding her meals. I think she fried liver and put out pickled herring or tripe because Dad wanted those, not to force us to eat that which made us gag.

I don't precisely recall the evening menu that elicited David's Freudian slip. Perhaps it was a salmon loaf. (He wasn't fond of fish.) David was nine or ten at the time and appeared to be picking at the food. Dad grew impatient and said, "Why aren't you eating?"

"It's good, but I don't like it," David replied.

LATER THAT YEAR I arrived home from a late basketball practice at Washington Junior High School. The rest of the family had eaten, and Mother left a platter for me on the table. I was ravenous, inhaling the fragrance of Mom's rich spaghetti sauce that Dad's sister, Aunt Mary Lombardi, had taught our Swedish mother to make.

Mom always shredded Parmesan cheese from a block, rather than purchase what we snobbishly referred to as "the canned stuff"— the pre-grated, chemical-infused product that came in green cardboard containers on unrefrigerated supermarket shelves.

Several months earlier Dad allowed Mom to hire Mary Hantz from the neighborhood to come in one day a week to iron clothes and help with cleaning. We'd also had spaghetti and meatballs last week and had not used all the pale, grated Parmesan, which Mom left in a small bowl. A few days before, she'd baked a coconut cream pie, and put the leftover shredded coconut in a similar bowl.

Mary discovered both dishes in the refrigerator and, assuming they were the same substance, combined them into one bowl, which was placed on the table to be sprinkled over that evening's pasta.

I sat down, mounded my plate with spaghetti and five or six meatballs, ladled on the cheese, and waded in.

Something wasn't right; I bit into noodles with cheese that hadn't melted. Further, it was chewy and sweet. I hollered, "Hey, this isn't cheese, it's coconut!"

Mother hurried into the kitchen and held a finger to her lips. "It's fine," she asserted in a restrained whisper. From his upstairs bedroom where he had begun his homework, David wailed, "See?"

In the living room with the evening paper, Dad was silent, though youngest brother Stephen said he observed Dad lying on the sofa and jostling the newspaper covering his abdomen, shaking with laughter he tried to stifle. While Dad was not known as a mirthful man, he had an infectious laugh when something amused him. He loved Jack Benny and wasn't above a very occasional prank. During our boyhood, Dad always gave us haircuts, saving money, of course, but also giving him an opportunity to tease us. I recall one time, during the run of Walt Disney's *Davy Crockett* television show, he gave David a cut that resembled a coonskin cap, with the back of David's head resembling the animal's tail. It took a couple of hours before David noticed; he wasn't happy, and before fixing it, Dad again struggled to keep control of his giggling.

Perhaps his best-remembered jape was the mid-1950s Fourth of July fireworks display that he promised all the neighbors on Bear Island in Island Lake, north of Duluth, where he had built his cabin. Many neighbors with young children were going to head back to the city to let the family enjoy the municipal firework show that evening. Dad convinced many to stay, promising a show of his own on his beach at 9:00 p.m.

Perhaps twenty-five or thirty adults and kids had assembled by 8:45, eager to see what Dad had arranged. Every few minutes Dad would tell the crowd to "hold on to your hats" because the show would get underway in just a bit. A minute or two past nine, Dad appeared on the beach with a railroad flare that he lit and stuck in the sand. "Fireworks," he announced and retreated to the cabin where, free of restraining his laughter, he sagged into the porch sofa and told Mother that his little lark was merely an April Fool jest three months late.

MY FATHER AND THE MOBSTER

The Americans are certainly hero-worshippers, and always
take their heroes from the criminal classes.

—Oscar Wilde

SEVERAL WEEKS AGO I eavesdropped on a conversation coming
from the next booth in a restaurant where I was eating lunch. A
gravel-voiced man was saying that his grandfather had served soft
drinks to Bonnie Parker and Clyde Barrow in Lakefield, Minnesota,
just before they robbed the bank at nearby Okabena in 1933. The fellow seemed pleased to relate this story, and his companion sounded
duly impressed as well. "Geez, Bonnie and Clyde," he said. "I never
knew they got up here to Minnesota."

I didn't either, and I waited for amplification, but someone else
joined the pair behind me, and the subject changed.

The awe in their voices when the men talked about the infamous
Bonnie and Clyde was palpable, bringing to mind an old college
chum who had attended elementary school in Fort Worth, Texas,
with Lee Harvey Oswald. Unlike so many who claim to have known
or encountered notorious persons, he had a class photograph for
proof. "Oswald was a kind of nonentity in school," my friend recalled,
but he seemed never to tire of relating his tenuous connection to
JFK's assassin.

IN THE 1970S, I was a volunteer with Amicus Inc., a Minnesota-
based organization that paired community volunteers with prison
inmates who would be eligible for parole within a year. The judge

who founded Amicus reasoned that if a con had a friend with no criminal history, the two could bond, and upon release the felon might be less inclined to return to old associates and commit future crimes leading to reincarceration.

Barney, the inmate to whom I was assigned at the time, had served sixteen nonconsecutive years for three armed robbery convictions. He claimed to know nearly every con who had served time in Minnesota's Stillwater prison from 1949 into the mid-1970s. One day in the visitor's lounge, he pointed out T. Eugene Thompson, a lawyer who'd been given a life sentence for hiring a hit man to murder his wife, Carol. This 1963 "murder of the century" case received international press coverage.

During my visit several months later, a shambling, bald con with a Roman nose, wearing inmate khakis, waved at Barney. "Hiya, Barn," he said before taking a seat nearby with his own visitor. "That's Rocky Lupino," Barney said almost reverently, adding, "He's a pal of mine."

Lupino's criminal history was extensive, and during the 1940s Minneapolis police called him the city's number one crime problem, with connections to mob syndicates. He shared media coverage with the city's other high-profile hoodlum, Isadore Blumenfeld (aka Kid Cann), though the latter was further up the crime ladder, engaging in white-collar enterprises with Meyer Lansky as well as murder and mayhem. Rocky Lupino wasn't above murder either, but he was arrested only for burglary until he was accused of participation in the disappearance and murder of Tony DeVito in September 1952. Lupino and John Azzone kidnapped DeVito and took him from Minnesota to Wisconsin where they allegedly strangled him and buried the body. DeVito had been an accomplice with Lupino and Azzone in a South Carolina burglary and was slated to testify against them during that trial.

Because DeVito's body was never located, the case stalled until 1960, when officials charged Lupino with kidnapping. He was convicted and sentenced to two to eighty years—a stretch he was serving when I encountered him.

I thought little of this until some weeks later when I was at my parents' home in Duluth and happened to mention my work with

Amicus. Since I knew that Lupino had been an infamous transgressor in Minnesota, I told Dad I'd once seen him in the Stillwater visitors' lounge.

Dad grunted. "Pa knew old man Lupino. Don't know if they met in Italy or where they got acquainted. The Lupinos used to come visit us in Duluth, and we went down to see them in Minneapolis a few times. There was one time up at our house when we sat down for dinner, the old man pulled a big revolver from his belt and set it on the dining room table. 'Per protezione,' he said. That's 'for protection' in Italian. I remember that everybody laughed. I was just a kid so I wondered why he thought he needed protection at our house. Later I realized he might have had something to do with the mob. I guess Rocky sort of followed his old man in that line. He was just a kid then, seven or eight years younger than me." Dad paused, seeming to reflect on his family's history with the Lupinos. "They were nice people," he went on. "But they didn't laugh like a lot of the other Italian families we knew. I don't know, maybe he did need protection down in Minneapolis."

Dad's anecdote interested me, and I contemplated asking Lupino if he remembered the Duluth Fedos the next time I saw Barney. But over the next several months Lupino was never present in the visitors' lounge when Barney and I were meeting, and Barney was paroled soon after, so the likelihood of my seeing Lupino again vanished. I had not heard his name mentioned in the thirty-plus years since his death (prior to his pending trial for the 1980 murder of a Skokie, Illinois, jeweler) until several months ago, when a man I have never met sent me an assemblage of small black-and-white snapshots dating to the 1920s and 1930s that he found in a box of miscellaneous items he had purchased at an estate auction. He thought it might be of interest to me because he'd noticed there were several pictures with the Fedo name written beneath them.

My wife and I began paging through the album, but the first half displayed only shots of people whose names and faces were totally unfamiliar. There were pictures of smiling children, of teenagers in football uniforms, of young adults leaning against automobiles, of sunbathers on beaches at Lake Minnetonka or Bass Lake. There were other photographs taken in Spring Park and elsewhere in southern

Minnesota, and I wondered where the Fedo connection might be. Our family's roots—after my paternal grandparents migrated from the southern Italian province of Calabria—were in northern Minnesota: Aurora and Duluth.

It was clear, however, that these photographs had belonged to a family of Italian-Americans. There were pictures with last names: DeMuse, Molinaro, Pagani, Mamone, Valentine. Some first names: Rocco, Tony, Dominic, Maria, Spazimina. There were numerous snapshots of one young woman alone or in the company of others. In the collection she is designated as "R." There's R with Isabel, R with Tony, R with Spaz. It seemed clear that the book had belonged to whoever R was.

Finally I came across a childhood photograph of my father and his boyhood neighbor Alec Sylvester. They are sitting together on a bench, dressed in cowboy suits replete with wooly chaps and Stetson hats. Alec's arms are folded across his abdomen; Dad has absently pointed a pistol at the camera. The boys appear to be about ten years old, and the photograph was taken in 1919. A turn of the page and there's Dad again, younger, perhaps eight and wearing outsize knickers. He's standing at the bottom of the back steps to the family's home in Duluth's Little Italy and holding a baritone horn.

There were more of Dad's family in the photograph album—my grandmother and a cluster of other Italian women in front of their house; my aunt Catherine appears in several poses, including one as the bride in her first marriage; the date underneath reads June 15, 1929. She is also in other pictures with R. Dad and his brother Frank, wearing tuxedos, are in Catherine's wedding tableau, and they also stand separately and jointly with R in a series of other wedding photographs.

Finally I learn R's identity from a newspaper announcement with a photograph of her own engagement dated October 5, 1924. Her name is Rose. And I'm caught short by the family cognomen—Lupino. This is Rose Lupino's photograph album.

Many of the pictures in Rose's album are of Rocco, her younger brother, as a grinning lad, happy in his familial surroundings; there is no hint here of the gangster he was to become. Portraits of family gatherings express togetherness, if not happiness, though in some boyhood snapshots of Rocky he exhibits a faint, enigmatic smile, and with the advantage of hindsight, one wonders if moments earlier he'd taken a measure of satisfaction by perhaps dispatching a stray cat. Viewing Rocco as a boy, I recalled a production of Norman Corwin's play *The World of Carl Sandburg* and a quote from the poet: "Schicklgruber too had a mother." This reference came from a section dealing with the joy a baby brings to a family and how even Hitler as a toddler may have been thought beautiful, filled with potential in the eyes of his single mother. Likewise Rocco Lupino's mother could not have anticipated the man who would evolve from the carefree lad in his sister's photograph collection. But in seeing the pictures and retracing Rocco's life in crime, I wanted to understand how and why my father's family had become intimate with the Lupinos.

IN THE EARLY TWENTIETH CENTURY, when immigrants from Southern Italy met with rather fierce discrimination, Italian gangs provided protection of sorts for residents of Little Italys around the country. Thus many of those labeled as mobsters by the rest of society were esteemed by their compatriots. The father of a daughter harassed at school might expect the neighborhood *padrone* to have local toughs thrash the harassers. Such an act earned loyalty from the avenged *famiglia*.

Might Signor Lupino have contributed this service in defense of one of my six aunts? Dad never said anything, and it seems unlikely, since Dad's people were in Duluth and the Lupinos lived in Minneapolis.

Did Dad and Uncle Frank date Lupino girls? Again, no evidence anywhere. Just these photographs of my people that I'd never seen before.

For the record, my father was what used to be called a pillar of the community. He worked his way through college cutting the hair of fellow students and faculty during the height of the Great Depression. It took him more than seven years to earn his degree, and he was the only one of nine children in his family to attend, let alone complete, post–high school education. He became a charter member of the Duluth Symphony Orchestra, taught industrial arts in Duluth schools for nearly forty years, serving a couple of terms as union president, and was on various boards and committees until his 1974 retirement. As far as I know he'd never been arrested—never even received a speeding ticket.

On the other hand, he wasn't unaware of things illicit. When he left high school he worked as a gofer and handyman for a small businessman in Duluth. One of his tasks was to drive female employees from one of the man's other establishments to downtown and pick them up several hours later. He eventually realized he was ferrying hookers to meet clients.

But this likely was his only involvement with the unseemly. Why did he even bother to mention his long-ago association with a hit man? Was it the urge to connect with celebrity, heedless of the celebrity's notoriety? For instance, how many Minnesotans of a certain age told grandchildren and acquaintances that they'd encountered John Dillinger when that Public Enemy Number 1 was hanging out in St. Paul?

I'd wager there are dozens of now-aging newsboys in Minneapolis who will claim Kid Cann used to buy papers from them and was a generous tipper. A restaurant owner from that era recalled that the Blumenfelds (Isadore and younger brother Yiddy) were worshipped by several generations of neighborhood boys.

My wife's grandfather, a religious conservative, liked to tell about building a house for Al Capone near Winter, Wisconsin, at the height of Scarface's fame.

And I admit that I must have told dozens of people about my chance rendezvous with T. Eugene Thompson and Rocco Lupino. These were vicarious brushes with underbelly luminaries. Was this my father's rationale for sharing his reminiscence with me? Dad died in 1999, and his surviving sisters—in their eighties and nineties now—are in various stages of memory loss, unable to enlighten me about what seems an odd and unlikely relationship.

Though my father was not easily impressed by status or personage, I think he was as fascinated by notable criminals as the rest of us. It's probably in our DNA. None of this supplies a definitive answer to my wondering about people in my family, whom I loved and respected, and their friendship with the Lupinos.

My father met many renowned artists from the classical music world who performed with the Duluth Symphony. I recall the names Robert Merrill, Risë Stevens, and Salvatore Baccaloni from the Metropolitan Opera. Dad once dined with and introduced the humorist and television host Sam Levenson to an educators' convention during Dad's tenure as president of the Northeast Minnesota Education Association. There were others, too, but the only one he ever singled out for elaboration was Rocky Lupino, the killer.

A FAMILY INFORMED BY
PYLORIC STENOSIS

ONE KINDERGARTEN MORNING Miss Geddes excused me to the boys' room, where I removed every stitch of raiment, including socks and shoes, folded the clothes, and placed them on a nearby bench before alighting on the commode. A few moments later classmate Jack Sharkey sauntered into the room heading for a bank of urinals. He noticed me and did a quick double take. "Where are your clothes?" I pointed to the bench. He looked at the garments, then back at me. After a moment he spoke again. "Gee, aren't you cold?"

Until Jack's reaction at finding a birthday-suited buddy on the throne, it never occurred to me that no one else toileted stark naked.

Prior to my third birthday I'd been diagnosed with pyloric stenosis, a malady that produces severe abdominal cramping caused when the sphincter muscle of the pylorus prevents passage of food into the duodenum. Statistically, fewer than three persons in one thousand are affected by the disorder, the majority of them firstborn males.

About the time I turned four, my parents instructed me to take off my clothes before toileting because I sometimes experienced simultaneous vomiting and diarrhea.

But beyond my epiphany after being seen undressed by Jack Sharkey, vestiges of pyloric stenosis continued to impact our family years later.

I AM FOUR YEARS OLD, sitting on Mother's lap in the Duluth Medical Arts Building office of Dr. Robert Peers Buckley, our pediatrician, who explains there's not much to be done for me. He speaks quietly to Mother and assures her that I'll very likely outgrow my condition by the time I turn nine or ten. Meanwhile he tells her to maintain a soothing atmosphere in the house, making sure I avoid stressful situations along with corn and other fiber-laden comestibles. Next year I would return for further tests and once again swallow tumblers of thick, foul-tasting barium for the ongoing x-rays of stomach and colon.

WHEN OUR FAMILY visited the homes of my parents' friends, the first order of business was to make certain I knew the location of the bathroom in case my stomach rumbled. "The doctor tells us that Mickey's disorder is also quite common in young puppies and foals," Mother offered one evening at her best friend's house. "I'm not sure why he said that." Neither was her friend.

I grew resourceful with others' awareness of my condition. Should something be brought to the table that did not meet my fancy—liver, canned asparagus, headcheese, or poached herring— I would excuse myself and lie on a davenport until the adults finished. Sometimes, thoughtful hosts would bring me a dish of vanilla ice cream to assuage the moaning and settle my stomach.

During my early elementary school years, Mother would contact teachers prior to the start of class and explain the situation. She wanted them to know that stress could exacerbate spasms, which in turn would result in summoning a janitor to hasten with mop and bucket.

She neglected, however, to bring this to the attention of the bus driver before he transported two dozen children, including me, to Lakeside Elementary School for our first day in kindergarten. The excited conversations of little kids must have nettled the driver because at one point he shouted, "Be quiet!" I hadn't uttered a sound, but now frightened, I upchucked on the floor, creating great pandemonium among those nearby. Classmates gave me wide berth throughout that first week of school and especially on the playground during recess, where one sandy-haired chap exclaimed, "Be careful around that kid 'cause he'll heave up on you."

Three weeks later our family moved to Jack Sharkey's East Hillside neighborhood where I transferred to U. S. Grant Elementary School.

THROUGHOUT MY EIGHT-YEAR SIEGE with pyloric stenosis, adults were most solicitous of my condition, carefully reviewing what I could and could not ingest. The latter included not only those items on the list Dr. Buckley gave Mother but also anything I didn't like. I was never forced to consume creamed cabbage, canned peas, or liver like my childhood playmates.

While younger brother David and my cousins were often directed to clean their plates in consideration of starving Chinese children, the dictum didn't apply to me. "How come the Chinese children don't starve when he doesn't eat everything?" David wailed over a supper of canned squash and fried tripe—a favorite of my Calabrese father's.

"I clean my plate," I replied, covering a smirk with my hand and wading into a dinner of soft-boiled egg, toast, and sugared banana slices.

Eventually this solicitous adult behavior over my health got the better of David, so he conjured stomach problems of his own. He was four years younger and began to complain of having terrible pains and just couldn't eat certain viands placed before him. Our parents were dismissive. "You're lucky you don't have real tummy-aches like your brother," Mother told him. "Please sit down and finish your dinner."

David persisted, but crying wolf almost did him in. A month later, when his appendix burst, it took a full day for him to convince anyone that he was in agony. Dr. Buckley told my mother that if she'd waited a few more hours before taking him to the emergency room at St. Luke's Hospital, he might not have survived. While recovering from surgery David contracted the mumps.

My pyloric spasms impacted the family in other areas as well. The excess attention I received contributed to David's insecurities. He began to worry that while we were outside playing, Mother would slip away and leave us, so he periodically abandoned play and raced home to ascertain her whereabouts. This practice got up Mother's nose after a while, and she'd occasionally ignore the little guy's calls to her, which increased his anxiety.

David also quickly determined that when I begged off performing household chores due to stomach issues that I was faking at least half the time, yet he was often required to complete those tasks.

An extremely bright fellow, David far exceeded my academic achievements, earning straight As all through elementary and secondary schools, but as soon as our aunts and uncles congratulated him, they'd turn to me and inquire about my health. The pattern continued for years after I was spasm-free.

David became valedictorian of his high school class, earned his doctorate, and has been an esteemed college administrator in Massachusetts and Singapore. I suspect my pyloric stenosis impelled him to succeed, to be noticed and valued, though he might have settled for more solicitude during his childhood. He never really had a chance to be the new baby because Mother continually fretted about my sensitive stomach.

During my teen years, Mother waited up to see that I was safely in the house after an evening out. She never did that with David, claiming he had no propensity for mischief and could be trusted implicitly. Instead of basking in her trust, I think the adolescent David would have much preferred our mother waiting for him at evening's end with a hug.

Referencing Dr. Buckley's advice about avoiding stress in my presence, our parents tried not to argue. Disagreements festered, however, producing periods of unspoken rage, sometimes broken only by Mother's tears. This troubled David and me, though neither of us spoke of it until we were in our thirties. Our father, whose Italian familial tendency toward depression was manifest, seemed unable or unwilling to discuss it with our Swedish-German mother, and days passed in sullen, stony silence.

When I was nearly twelve, youngest brother Stephen was born, and for a while he also had a queasy stomach syndrome. As we used to say when he was a little tyke, he'd upchuck even *before* the proverbial hat dropped. He didn't inherit pyloric stenosis but rather experienced what Dr. Buckley called "a nervous gut." I was unsympathetic and cured him when he was four by threatening him during a week our parents were attending an educator's convention in San Juan. I told him if he vomited anywhere at any time, he would have to clean up after himself. Our family wasn't big enough for more than one victim of digestive distress, and I had dibs on it.

Because our parents eschewed arguments due to my condition, their overall communication was repressed. Their grievances with each other mostly went unspoken, though Mother occasionally confided in me when vexed by something Dad said or did. For rapprochement with Dad, she relied on Stephen from the time he was six years old. Mom would approach him with something like "See if your father would like to go on a picnic after church." Stephen would carry the message and return with a reply. At the time I never associated any of this with my affliction.

Early on I developed a strategy to deal with the stress that might trigger spasms. I trained myself to doze before events in which I participated. As our Central High School football team was bused to the stadium where we played conference games, I'd sleep while my anxious teammates stewed. I also missed my first-act entrance on opening night in our senior class play while snoozing in a green room chair. I still nap to avoid confronting a current crisis or stress, which increases pressure on others involved.

SEVERAL YEARS AGO at a high school class reunion, friends were sharing stories of the old days, and somebody wondered whatever happened to Jack Sharkey. "I don't know," one fellow replied, "but one time he told me that way back in kindergarten, he saw Mike here taking a dump, naked as the day he was born." The group at our table cackled. "Why in hell would you take everything off?" someone demanded.

"He had pyloric stenosis," my wife replied, launching into the litany Dr. Buckley gave my mother decades earlier, including the curious information about puppies and foals. I excused myself and ordered another beer.

Twenty-two years after Mother died, my father terminally abed and not always connected to the present, one day out of the blue he asked how my stomach had been lately. I told him I hadn't had any problems since junior high school.

He seemed not to have heard me. "You came awfully close to being spoiled. Did you know I had the same thing when I was little? Nobody paid any attention. There were nine kids at our house, remember, and we didn't have time or money for getting sick. That damn stomach of yours." He paused for a moment. "It caused all kinds of tension in this house, and that was the last thing you were supposed to have."

THE UNMAKING
OF A MISSIONARY

ONE MID-NOVEMBER SATURDAY when I was twelve, I was sent next door by Mother to borrow a cup of sugar from Grandma. I'd barely entered the kitchen with the empty measuring cup when Aunt Hilma came in waving an envelope at me and smiling. "Got a letter yesterday from Reuben," she announced.

I was not much interested in the missive from Reuben, a missionary our church sponsored in Siam. Hilma took all of life seriously but nothing more so than her religion. She belonged to a Swedish Baptist church, making her an outsider among others of her predominantly Lutheran nationality. Hilma regarded Lutherans as an apostate lot, charging that Lutherans had cheated her father out of his considerable holdings in Sweden, forcing the family to emigrate in ignominious penury to America in 1897.

She never married; her church became her passion. She received letters from Reuben because she faithfully mailed him a five-dollar check each month from her own meager earnings as a seamstress. Beyond this, however, she always insisted that I become a missionary too. She inevitably read Reuben's letters to me shortly after they arrived, encouraging me to emulate the sainted Reuben.

"Vouldn't it be vunderful," she said, beaming, her eyes moist behind her trifocals, "If vun day you could be a missionary in Siam vit Reuben?"

I nodded dully, and she went on about the seminary in St. Paul I'd attend, reminding me that cousin Jimmy went there and was a minister in Sacramento. "It's fine to be a minister," she said, "but it is nutting compared to a missionary who vorks vit headens in da yungles."

It wasn't my intention to work with jungle heathens, but I couldn't tell that to my great aunt. Instead, she discovered that by herself the next day.

The family attended Bethel Baptist Church, but I rarely sat with them during services. Instead I sat with my friend David Olson and with a thirtyish man named Les, who was a spastic. Les's body and face were contorted and his speech somewhat slurred, but he was readily accepted by younger kids in the congregation. He possessed a keen mind and was an excellent chess player. His sense of humor, however, was sophomoric, which explained his appeal to David and me. He used to tell us slightly ribald jokes during sermons, sending us dashing from the sanctuary stifling giggles and drawing stern stares from adults.

In time we moved our seating to the balcony, a haunt usually reserved for parents with young children who might require nursery tending. The church nursery was attached behind the balcony. But since several volunteers minded the nursery, parents most often returned downstairs, leaving the balcony nearly vacant, except for young boys with fractious intentions.

Services at church normally ended about noon, with the congregation growing restless whenever the pastor's sermon overran that hour. But that Sunday our minister was out of town, and a visiting evangelist took his place. It became apparent to all present, as the noon hour approached, that the evangelist wasn't winding down but in fact just getting started. "I know I'm running a bit long this morning, but the Lord has laid this burden on my heart. . . ."

Ten minutes later he asked us to please bear with him a few more minutes. At 12:30 he repeated his plea and fervently bore on. At 12:45 he raised his arms. "Oh, people, do you hear the message this morning?"

Les, his face hot with anger and frustration, stood in the second row of the balcony. "Ahh, shit," he bellowed, then stalked out of the balcony and clomped down the stairs.

David and I crimsoned and slipped down the back stairs where Les was zipping his jacket near the cloakroom. A few other adults were retrieving their coats and boots, offering weak, embarrassed smiles. "My pork roast is about to burn," said one woman as she picked up a camel-colored coat. "But wasn't his message thrilling?"

"You're crazy," Les snarled.

David and I had stifled ourselves too long by then, and we began to laugh as the woman departed. We clutched thick wool coat sleeves and stuffed them into our mouths to keep our eruptions from being heard in the sanctuary. I slid to the floor, tears coursing down my cheeks. David suddenly sobered, held his belly, snorted another laugh, and began to retch. He grabbed a man's large over-shoe and vomited into it.

I pounded the floor limply, my abdomen in spasms. David was still hunched over the boot when we heard the organ strike the opening chords of "The Doxology," signaling the merciful end of the service. I scrambled to my feet and tugged at David. "We've got to get out of here," I said.

We made it into the foyer and down the stairs into the men's room, where David took a long drink and I splashed water on my face and cleared my throat. I started giggling again, and David grabbed me.

"Don't. I'm sick," he said. "I can't take any more."

We went upstairs then. The cloakroom filled with parishioners struggling into wraps and boots. While searching for my own coat, I saw a man slip into the overshoe that David had used. There was a suctiony, gurgling sound as his booted foot contacted the floor.

"Well, what in the world?" he murmured, extracting the offended shoe from the boot. "What's this? What in the world is this?" he asked of no one in particular.

"Golly, I hope it isn't what I think it is," a woman said, wrinkling her nose.

"Who would do a thing like this?" the man said as he carefully kicked off the shoe and worked his sock loose. "My goodness, I'm a mess."

This was too much for me, and I dashed outside and pressed a handful of snow against my head to keep from laughing again. David slumped against the side of his father's station wagon and held his sides.

Seated around Grandma's Sunday dinner table an hour or so later, Hilma announced, "I know something, and I'm ashamed."

My father, who seldom attended church, looked absently at her. "What would that be?"

"Some boys made a commotion at church dis morning."

"Shush, Hilma," said Grandma, who didn't like the tone of Hilma's voice.

"I von't shush, Gustie," she said. "I von't shush, even though I'm ashamed."

"If you're going to tell us about Mickey throwing up in Abner Swanson's boot this morning, forget it," Uncle Howard said. "Nobody needs to know a thing like that at the dinner table."

"What?" my mother said, dropping her salad fork in her coffee cup.

"I didn't throw up," I said. "David Olson did. Was he supposed to vomit on the floor?"

"Uff—Mickey," said Aunt Hilma, shaking her head. "Maybe you shouldn't be tinking about being a missionary yet. Vat sort of headen would listen to a boy who goes to church and womits in anodder man's owershoe?"

THE HILL

DULUTHIANS DO NOT HAVE adversarial relationships with their hills. Hills are simply there, like the lake, and provide no undue cause for concern—even in winter. The exception is one western end peak that bedeviled several generations of Italian Americans.

During the years of my father's growing up and well beyond, my grandparents, Sam and Amelia Fedo, lived at 317 Seventeen-and-one-half Avenue West. This street is scarcely more than one block long, but it is situated on a heart-breakingly steep slope. In those pre-salt-on-roads winters, it was insurmountable by auto and in icy conditions required herculean efforts to ascend on foot. Sometimes the hill resembled a Matterhorn summit as crews of neighbors attempted to scale her heights. Tugging, pushing one another, grown men and women on hands and knees inched their way up the hill, hollering encouragement now and again or cursing in frustration as a foothold was lost, sending one cascading down on his back, feet flailing in the air.

Often the slide didn't end at the bottom of the hill, which butted against West Third Street. This too, was a terrifyingly long hill, dropping down another quarter mile until it intersected with Piedmont Avenue.

Part of the hill's history belongs to my great-uncle Franco Fulci. He migrated to America from the perennially impoverished Italian province of Calabria, and with no residence of his own, he stayed with my grandparents and their nine children.

One morning he hopped on a bicycle and started a slow descent down Seventeen-and-one-half Avenue West. Suddenly the chain slipped off, and he found himself plummeting down the hill at frightening speed. Somehow he managed to negotiate the turn onto Third

Street, but instead of turning left up the hill, which would have brought him to a stop, he angled right, whipping around the corner and quickly exceeding forty miles an hour. His terror-wrought shriek dropped neighbors' jaws and elicited signs of the cross from women on the hill. He continued down, demonstrating remarkable dexterity as the bike battered onto the streetcar ruts and rails on Piedmont, pitching him forward onto the bike's crossbar.

Those witnessing the ride said at that point he was ashen, his eyes narrowed with pain. The harrowing descent continued another mile before he came to rest near what is now Wheeler Field in West Duluth. The bike withstood the hammering better than he, and when he returned home, he refused to discuss the misadventure. Some said a man with lesser biking skills would never have survived.

Franco was not interested in plaudits, however, and only wanted assurance that he was capable of fathering children. Several weeks later he was on a boat back to Italy, never to return to America or the peril of her hills.

Another time, perhaps twenty years later, my father stepped out the door one evening on his way to a symphony rehearsal and slipped off the steps, releasing his French horn, which rapidly clattered down the hill. Giving chase, my father remained about a half block behind the instrument, which neatly rounded the corner at Third Street (as had Uncle Franco) and clanked its way toward Piedmont.

Dad was now managing only two or three steps at best before performing belly and back flops; he righted himself and repeated the process until the instrument plowed into a high snowbank, and he caught it. It was relatively undamaged, though its case was nicked and gouged. Dad suffered injuries mainly to his pride and derriere, and, excellent athlete that he was, charged back up the hill, got into his car, and wasn't even late for the rehearsal.

My grandmother, a sturdily constructed Calabrese, thought nothing of the hill and uncomplainingly hauled her weekly groceries, purchased in the West End, up both the long Third Street climb and Seventeen-and-one-half Avenue West. Her children often carped though, especially if they'd returned and were told to go back for something else. Two trips like that could consume the better part of a day.

Some years later, about 1948 or 1949, after Grandma had died, my dad's sister Mary and her husband, Dominic Lombardi, came to live with Grandpa in the speckled brown-shingled house at the top of the hill. Dominic stepped out one morning after an overnight sleet storm. He got one hand on the handle of his car door, groped with the other for his keys, and let go of the door. He spun and began to slide. He remained on his feet, though out of control, for nearly half a block. Then he bounced down but landed upright and, skidding as he rounded the corner, continued down Third Street. Finally he was stopped by the streetcar tracks of Piedmont.

After picking himself up and deciding he wasn't hurt, Dominic noticed his next-door neighbor shivering in a satin bathrobe. One foot was bare and chilled blue; the other wore a cloth carpet slipper. His hand was slightly cut, and a coffee-cup handle was looped around his thumb.

"What are you doing here?" Dominic asked.

"I was having a cup of coffee," the neighbor explained. "Just went out on the porch to get the paper." He needed no further explanation.

The hill had won again.

DISCOVERING RITA

ONE WINTER EVENING back in 1959 or 1960, I was sitting in the announcer's booth at KDAL-AM, a radio station in Duluth, visiting with Loren Sandquist, who had recently landed a night shift as a disc jockey. Loren had been the program director at KUMD, the student-run station at the University of Minnesota–Duluth, when I joined the staff as a freshman announcer a couple of years earlier. Loren possessed what used to be called a radio voice—deep, mellifluent, resonant. He was one of the first alumni of the campus station to land a professional broadcast gig. He appreciated having folks from the old college crew visit during late-night programming, as he was the only person in the facility after 11:00 p.m. He told me that he and a couple of other KDAL jocks had been receiving phone calls from a local woman named Rita, offering sexual favors.

Loren had taped one of her calls to him, which he played for me that evening. Over and over she repeated she was in love with Loren's voice and had tried visiting him during his shift on several occasions but always found the outside door to the station locked. She told him to name the time and unlock the door so she could finally see him. She was, she said, eager to meet and please him as she had other local celebrities, naming several.

Loren said nobody at the station knew her age or what she looked like, but figured the woman was "a bit off her rocker."

ONE EARLY SEPTEMBER MORNING in 1951, Ray Ignatius, the boys' gym teacher at Washington Junior High School, had the forty-plus boys in his third-hour class line up in alphabetical order around the perimeter of the gymnasium. I didn't pay close attention until I heard the name George Fedo. George Fedo—who was that, I wondered? Then my name was called and I was placed next to this George fellow. Ray looked at both of us and said, "Are you boys related?" I had never seen George before, but now we looked into each other's face and shrugged. Ray moved on.

George had the black hair and olive skin of my Dad's Calabrese family, while I bore the lighter hair and skin tone of my mother's Scandinavian-German lineage. I'd never before heard George's name uttered among the score of my father's cousins who lived in Duluth and Aurora, Minnesota, and Detroit.

Later that day around the dinner table, I asked Dad if we were related to a kid named George Fedo. Dad sighed and said we'd talk about it some other time.

Over the course of the school year I grew more acquainted with George, though we weren't friends. He lived several miles from my neighborhood, and I never asked him about his family. About halfway through the school year I heard he was in foster care. Dad again put off discussing George.

I DIDN'T SEE GEORGE in the halls during the first weeks of the eighth-grade school year, so I asked one of his friends where he was. "He's gone to Boys Town," the kid said. "I think it's in Nebraska."

That evening at dinner I told Dad that George Fedo was in Boys Town, and again I asked whether we were related.

Dad put down his fork, dabbed his mouth with his napkin, and slowly nodded. "Well, he was Theresa's boy."

I had never heard Theresa's name either and asked who she was. "Tom and Sunta's sister."

I knew Tom pretty well, knew he was Dad's cousin who used to stop by the house from time to time. I'd met Sunta also but didn't see her often. I hadn't heard Theresa's name mentioned in any home of Fedo relatives, and now Dad was about to tell me why.

"Theresa wasn't quite right in the head," he said, tapping his temple. "She had a lot of problems." He paused; it was clear he didn't want this conversation. "Anyway, she got herself pregnant. Some fellow took advantage of her because she had mental issues. There was no way she could have taken care of a baby, so the doctor told her it died during childbirth." He paused again. "You don't know Theresa, do you? No reason why you should. She caused a lot of problems for her family. But she certainly couldn't take care of a child, so the county took it from her, and that was the boy you knew."

Dad said that Boys Town was the best thing that could have happened to George because if he'd stayed around Duluth, sooner or later Theresa would find out and there would be big trouble. It was better that he was finally away from Duluth, better for George and certainly better for Theresa.

FAST FORWARD TO CHRISTMAS 1962. I'm not home in Duluth. Instead I'm spending the holiday season in Omaha, Nebraska, performing at the Crooked Ear coffeehouse as one half of a folk-singing duo. An old family friend from Duluth, Jo-Jo Vatalaro, had recently taken a job in Boys Town as a counselor. He came to a midweek show and invited my partner, Dan Kossoff, and me to join him for breakfast at Boys Town on Saturday morning. He'd also give us a tour of the place.

During breakfast with Jo-Jo and several colleagues, one of them said, "It seems to me there was a Fedo kid here a while back. He related to you?"

"George Fedo?"

"Yeah, that's it. George. Nice kid. Joined the navy right after he graduated, I think."

Until Boys Town I hadn't given any thought to George or what might have happened to him; I'd immersed myself in high school athletics, social life, college, and the teaching job that awaited. But now I wondered again about George and, following the Omaha trip, told Dad that when Dan and I played there, we'd gone to Boys Town to see Jo-Jo Vatalaro and that a friend of his remembered George Fedo.

Dad frowned. "He was in Duluth last summer. Came with his wife and wanted to find his family—his mother, in particular." He shook his head. "Seemed like a real nice fella when we had him up to the lake. He remembered you, wondered what you were up to.

Tom's people were quite upset though, didn't know how to handle this and keep Theresa from knowing. Anyway Tony (Cousin Sunta's husband) told George that he would be better off not knowing about his mother. I think they sort of implied that Theresa had moved away a long time ago and was probably dead. Actually, they thought if Theresa knew George was alive, she'd have just gone crazy and maybe have to be put in an institution."

I said that George deserved to know the family, regardless of Theresa, whom I would meet for the first time six months later.

"THERESA WILL BE THERE," Dad said, referring to the large family gathering at Birch Lake, near Aurora. "You can't say a thing to her about George. She doesn't know and her family wants to keep it that way."

Theresa was a short, dark-haired, rather plain-looking woman who seemed to be in her early to midforties. My exchanges with her were brief. However, she certainly did not have Down syndrome, as had been implied over the years. Throughout the day I thought of George, who should have been present, regardless of the family concerns. He was entitled to his history, no matter how unseemly.

THERESA DIED a dozen years later. Not yet sixty, she had married a retired railroad man a decade earlier. By all accounts she'd been a dedicated wife.

Since Theresa was no longer in the picture, I attempted to contact George to give him genealogical information. I did periodic Google searches for him, but none of the George Fedos I found and wrote to were my cousin. Most of these Fedos, I learned, weren't Italian but rather Russian or Czech, using a shortened Fedo rather than the Fedorczak, Fedoroffsky, or Fedorova of their forebears.

Off and on I Googled the name for nearly ten years without success, writing to almost a dozen George Fedos without locating the Duluth native.

Just before Thanksgiving several years ago, my brother David, living in Singapore, forwarded me an e-mail from a woman named

Ally Fedo. She had found David's e-mail address when she Googled the Fedo cognomen. Her husband was Andrew Fedo, son of the late George Fedo, and Andrew was interested in locating family. All he knew was that George had been born in Duluth, Minnesota. Ally and Andrew were living in New Mexico.

David said he thought he remembered me mentioning George Fedo a time or two during our old Duluth days.

I responded to Ally's e-mail, informing her I had known George and wondered whatever became of him. He had died in his sixties, Ally wrote back, saying that her husband was thrilled to find family and hoped to meet everyone soon. Contacting long-lost relatives, she said, was the best possible Christmas present for Andrew, who was in his early forties.

That spring cousins gathered at our home to welcome Andrew into the family, and last summer we hosted a large Fedo family reunion in Duluth. Andrew, Ally, and their kids attended along with about sixty other cousins from a dozen states. Many cousins were getting acquainted for the first time.

But there was an intriguing conversation with one of George's first cousins, during which Theresa's name came up. "Grandpa was so ashamed because of her," he said. "Her promiscuity and all—disappearing for days at a time—just broke his heart. We think there was another child too that was taken from her as well. Nobody seems to know the name of that one, but I remember folks talking about it when I was a kid." He said Theresa would probably be considered a vulnerable adult today.

"There was this radio announcer in town," he continued. "Theresa was in love with him—actually just his voice. I don't think she ever met him. But she all the time said that he was her boyfriend.

"At about the same time she said she was changing her name. She idolized Rita Hayworth, the big movie star, and told everyone if anybody called Grandpa's house asking for Rita, it wasn't a wrong number, it was for her."

THE GRAND PIANO SMELT

THERE USED TO BE a rite of spring in Duluth that has diminished somewhat over recent decades. When the winter ice left the shorelines along Lake Superior and the St. Louis Bay, thousands of area residents used to break out chest waders, dip nets, and seines to catch buckets of silvery smelt for an annual fish fry.

I was nine when my father first let me accompany him across the Aerial Lift Bridge to Minnesota Point where I would participate in the smelt run. Crowds would gather evenings in late March or early April at Minnesota Point or where North Shore rivers emptied into Lake Superior. Everyone believed that the run began at dark. The surge of these small fish, however, was not dependent on darkness, because one particularly warm day in late March, I drove to the Lester River to sit on the rocks and read my political science assignment. No one else, save a young boy and his dog, was present. The mouth of the Lester was choked with the shimmering silver of smelt. So great were their numbers that some of them could not find room in the river and were flipping above the water's surface. The lad on the opposite side of the stream was swatting spawning smelt onto the shore with his hand while his dog barked at the flopping fish.

But I digress. After an early supper, Dad had younger brother David and me put on long underwear and winter gear. We would meet our neighbors, the Hassingers, at Mr. Hassinger's father-in-law's home, where smelting equipment was stored.

The smell of wood smoke hung heavy over Minnesota Point. Dozens of bonfires burned along the beaches on both sides of the Point—the lake and the bay. Kids poked sticks holding hot dogs or marshmallows into flames, heightening the festive atmosphere.

Over the years, an increasing number of smelters, imbibing and causing varying degrees of mayhem, resulted in fighting and destruction of property. There were a few drownings too, and the sport's appeal declined in later years, not so much because there were fewer smelt to be caught but because residents grew weary of boisterous late-night revelry in their neighborhoods. Many Park Pointers had snow fences ripped out of the sand to be used for bonfires. Others complained about unruly types urinating in their yards. Also, there were fish dumpers: people who filled pick-up truck beds with smelt and drove a few miles away before it occurred to them that it would take hours to clean their booty. Under cover of darkness, many loads of smelt were deposited along roadways—especially the Miller Trunk Highway—or even residential streets and alleys. But these incidents weren't prevalent until years later, about the time I moved away from Duluth.

On that first night there were small hip waders for us boys, and we manned the shoreside of the net while our fathers made the sweep from deeper water.

After about a dozen passes our fathers let us boys take the net ourselves, provided we remained in shallow water. Dad and Mr. Hassinger anticipated that we boys wouldn't catch many smelt in the shallow water of the St. Louis Bay, but we were unlikely to slip on a dropoff there.

Dick Hassinger and I didn't capture many smelt, but on one pass, as we hoisted the net, a large northern pike rolled out and began swimming parallel to the shore in a few inches of water rather than heading for the deep. Dick and I chased after him; I dropped to my knees, landing on and mortally wounding the leviathan of more than twelve pounds. The regular fishing opener was nearly two months away, and in Minnesota it was, and is, illegal to capture a game fish with your hands, and the regulation probably extends to the knees as well.

Dad and Mr. Hassinger discussed the matter a few moments, observing that the fish was breathing its last, and determined we should lug the pike up to Dick's grandfather's yard and place it by the back porch where it was unlikely game wardens would come looking for evidence of poaching.

Later that evening Dick and I brought in a net void of smelt but with two medium-sized walleyed pike, which we wanted to keep as well, but the fathers weren't going to be party to multiple violations. "We might bail you boys out of the pokey for the northern," my father said. "But you'll stay there overnight if you don't put those walleyes back."

As we prepared to depart an hour or so later, Dad withdrew a knife and filleted the northern, giving half to the Hassingers while we took the other. Each bony fillet was large enough to feed a family of four.

Though there were numerous smelting excursions during my boyhood, only one other was memorable. It occurred one evening during my junior year at the University of Minnesota–Duluth. Our Beta Phi Kappa fraternity had scheduled its annual smelting party to be held down at the end of Minnesota Point. We were to invite dates to participate in the event, which consisted of very little smelting; frat boys, then as now, held distinct predilections for beer. There was also the inevitable bonfire with hot dogs and marshmallows and the singing of "Kumbaya" and other au courant folk tunes accompanied by a half dozen or so guys who brought guitars. Nobody brought gear for smelting.

Except for my pal Dan Kossoff and me. We would shortly team up as a folk duo, performing in coffeehouses and on campuses for a couple of years. But this night we were double-dating two freshmen nursing students we'd fetched from their dormitory on Tenth Avenue East and Third Street, a few strides below St. Luke's Hospital. Dan and I had brought waders, and I borrowed Dad's seine, which turned out to be the only one representing a fraternity of more than forty men. We insisted on venturing into the lake for some fish. Neither of our dates were interested in smelting.

Dan and I made a single pass with the seine, scooping out a dozen or so smelt. Lacking a bucket in which to keep the fish, we put them on a paper plate.

An hour or so later, "Kumbaya"-weary, we returned our quite bored young ladies to their dorm. As we entered the lounge, Dan offered the girls our plate of smelt. Both wrinkled their noses. "Ish, what would we do with those?" one said.

"Cook 'em. Eat 'em," I said. "They're good."

"Ish," she repeated, and both girls exited.

Now the lounge was empty, except for Dan and me and a baby grand piano that dominated the room. Dan and I looked at each other. Neither of us spoke; I lifted the top on the grand and Dan put the paper plate of smelt inside. I carefully lowered the top and we left.

A week later a very angry St. Luke's dormitory housemother was barking at me over the telephone. "What were you thinking?" she bellowed. There had been a terrible odor for a couple of days in the lounge, and who would ever think to look inside a piano? The night before, one of the residents—probably a girl with receding olfactory senses—sat down to play, and the initial chord sounded strangely squishy. It wasn't the least bit funny, snarled the housemother when I guffawed. We were lucky that the piano wasn't damaged. Furthermore, neither I nor my friend would ever be allowed on those premises again. And she had a good mind to call the university dean, and it wouldn't surprise her if we were suspended from school.

Either she never phoned the dean, or the incident amused him as much as it did Dan and me. We were not suspended or even notified of the housemother's complaint.

But neither Dan nor I ever dated a student nurse again.

COUSIN JEAN

I WAS TWENTY-FIVE YEARS OLD before I first met my mother's cousin Jean in April 1965, but I had long been aware of her mythic status among Duluth relatives. She had left home years before and had made her mark in New York, counting that city's movers and shakers among her friends and acquaintances.

I had journeyed to New York specifically to see Jean. Several months before I would graduate with an MA degree in broadcast journalism from Kent State University, my mother reminded me that her cousin had many important connections in New York and might be willing to help me arrange interviews at major networks. When I phoned from Ohio, Jean said she'd be delighted to have me visit.

We met in her masculine oak-paneled office with dark leather chairs and sofas on the Avenue of the Americas, where she was vice president of a large public relations firm. "You remind me of your mother," Jean said, extending her hand. "When I was a little girl I thought she was beautiful. She should have gone to Hollywood." She paused to light a cigarette, exhaled, and smiled. "But then, of course, I wouldn't be talking to you right now, would I?"

She sat behind her desk, and began a strange and rambling reminiscence about her long-ago Minnesota days, recounting her first affair with a young Minneapolis newspaper reporter named Feike Feikema, who later wrote critically acclaimed novels under the name Frederick Manfred. She followed that with a story about another brief liaison with the novelist James T. Farrell, when he was a visiting lecturer at the University of Minnesota. She said she was barely eighteen during both of those affairs, and that upon learning of them her mother's sisters tried to lash her with a horsewhip.

From the bottom drawer of her desk, she produced a manila folder containing reviews of Manfred's books. "He's gone on to do wonderful work," she said. "Farrell, of course, was on the way down when I knew him. To tell the truth, I really wasn't much of a Studs Lonigan fan."

Jean also mentioned that she had married her third husband eight years ago, though they had lived separately for the last five. "Mother and my aunts were partly right," she said. "I was a sinner, but I didn't do anything wrong."

THROUGHOUT MY 1940S AND 1950S CHILDHOOD, Jean seldom visited Minnesota, even though her young son, Daniel, lived with Uncle Carl and Aunt Myrna on their farm near Mora. This apparent abandonment of the boy was barely mentioned; it was simply attributed to the way Jean was.

As perceived by Great Aunt Hilma, Jean was pretty, and no good could come of this. Pretty was not a desirable quality for a young woman raised among rural fundamentalists—especially her dogmatic aunts. And Jean was not only pretty but also smart and talented. As a youngster she used to perform a dead-on mimicry of Mae West's signature line: "Come up and see me sometime." It wasn't the line that worried relatives; it was little Jean's comprehension of the vamp. This child would require close supervision. Naturally enough, Jean found the vigilance stultifying. She rebelled in the only avenues open in the late 1930s: she read Sinclair Lewis and smoked cigarettes.

Jean's father, Dan, favored a laissez-faire approach toward his daughter's perspicacity and probing intellect. He was a man of perpetual middle age, who was unable to maintain steady employment. Whenever minor strife manifested itself at work, Dan's sensitive stomach rebelled, rendering him useless. He would either quit the job or be terminated. He had no propensity for conflict and thus was browbeaten by his wife and her four sisters, who regularly reminded him of his inadequacies. The women tolerated him because he served for many years as usher at the local Baptist church and eschewed alcohol. On several occasions throughout her adolescence, he told Jean he was proud of her but cautioned against divulging this to her mother and aunts.

As family breadwinner, Jean's mother placed her daughter under her sisters' charge, not trusting Dan to exercise appropriate discipline. When she was a high school senior, Jean won first prize in a national essay competition sponsored by the *Atlantic Monthly*. It was no surprise that the aunts discouraged her from mentioning the award. There was no sense adding pride and conceit to the list of evils impelling an adolescent girl toward perdition. But Jean's English teacher brought the accomplishment to the attention of a newspaper columnist who wrote a feature story on the gifted writer for the *Minneapolis Tribune*.

Jean's essay was a mild indictment of the stifling and sometimes abusive environment in which she lived. Airing an unflattering portrait of decent farm folk for an East Coast journal surely meant further drifting from the bedrock of homely values in which she had been raised. For this transgression, she was thrashed by two of her aunts. The award, however, carried a prize of several hundred dollars, which Jean used to purchase gifts for her parents, saving enough to buy herself a new pair of saddle shoes.

Meanwhile, Feikema had seen Jean's picture in the *Tribune* and had read her essay. His phone call to her and discussion of her work and his own literary aspirations evolved into her brief affair with this towering, fledgling novelist. Both he and Farrell critiqued Jean's writing and encouraged her. But following failure to place several other stories and essays in the *Atlantic Monthly*, she grew discouraged and put her publication hopes on hold.

DOWNING TUMBLERS OF CUTTY SARK and chain-smoking Camels on that languid New York afternoon, Jean said she would talk to friends at NBC about me. She also knew people at CBS. "I can't promise anything, but you have to understand that with a master's degree, you'd only be a page at NBC. At CBS you'll begin in the mail room. Of course, if you're still paging or sorting mail after six months, you're probably not going anywhere with networks, so you might have to look for a teaching job."

I assured her I would make the most of any opportunity, and she agreed to make some calls first thing Monday morning. As our session wore on, and she was well into her cups, Jean talked about her out-of-wedlock impregnation by a geology professor when she was twenty. Following oaths of recrimination by her aunts, she married the professor just prior to Daniel's birth. The marriage proved a bad one, and they soon divorced. The business of pregnancy and divorce scandalized the family, so everyone was relieved when Jean agreed to leave Daniel with Carl—the relative she both loved and respected. "He was the only man strong enough to stand up to those sisters," Jean said, adding she loathed Myrna. "She was a bitch." Jean looked at me, gauging my reaction to her pronouncement about an aunt the rest of the family had esteemed for her generosity. Myrna had often ministered to sick relatives, sometimes staying in their homes during illnesses, cleaning their houses and cooking.

"But I was alone then," Jean said, "and I thought things would be better for Daniel on the farm. I still think I was right."

After moving to New York, she found employment as a speechwriter at a large public relations concern and was crowned Miss Empire State Building a few months later. Her PR career flourished. She traveled the world and rose to vice president of the firm—a remarkable ascendancy for a woman in the 1950s. She showed me clips of articles—mostly inspirational and devotional—she ghostwrote for corporate executives from Fortune 500 companies. These had been published in *Colliers, Saturday Evening Post,* and *Reader's Digest.* Of Jean's more than two hundred published articles, not one carried her byline, and I asked if she ever resented being a ghostwriter.

She laughed. "My boss always says if you're going to prostitute yourself, make damn sure you're well-compensated." She gestured toward a Manet painting hanging on the wall behind her desk. "And I have been."

The conversation drifted then; Jean made small talk about the family in Minnesota and returned to Daniel, the son she left behind.

I had seen him more recently than she. Two years before, when I was awaiting discharge from the Air Force, Daniel showed up in uniform at the office one day. He had just arrived as a communications specialist at the base I was abandoning for a brief career as a middling folksinger before heading to graduate school. I hadn't seen him since he visited Duluth when he was eight and I was nine. I wouldn't have recognized him. Back then he was an awkward kid who batted cross-handed and cried on the softball field when a pop fly caromed off his chin. Now Daniel was tall and sinewy. He chain-smoked Camels. He never mentioned his mother. I told Jean about that encounter, avoiding Daniel's omission of her in our conversation. Jean stared out the window, not speaking.

Then she turned around and poured another drink. Jean did not arrange interviews for me. I was leaving New York on Tuesday, and my phone messages to her on Monday were not returned. A receptionist said Jean was away from her desk. I suspected she was hungover. Frustrated, I went back to Ohio and waited to hear from Jean. At week's end I wrote, thanking her for her efforts on my behalf, but she never responded, and indeed, I ended up with a teaching position.

During the next several years, whenever Jean's name came up during family dinners, I seethed. There were reports of her journeys to London and Cairo to develop projects for clients. If only she had followed through for me back in 1965, I might have progressed in the profession I had once fancied as a foreign correspondent. Instead I earned $6,000 a year teaching courses in radio and television to sophomores at a small Ohio college.

OVER TIME BOOZE and bad relationships despoiled Jean's professional and personal life. A distant relative informed us that the owner of the agency where Jean was vice president had sold the business a few years earlier, and Jean's position had been eliminated. She had also gone through treatment for alcoholism and suffered a broken hip. Not able to afford her posh Midtown apartment, Jean was renting a tiny room in Brooklyn, scrounging occasional freelance assignments from old acquaintances.

Then in the spring of 1985 she came to Minneapolis where I lived and taught. A stroke had hospitalized her mother. Several months later, following her mother's death, Jean called and asked me to be a pallbearer at the funeral. I was out of town, however, so she left the message on my answering machine. Her voice was youthful, energetic. She said she was sorry to have missed me but was returning to New York in a few days, eager to work. In fact, Jean remained in her mother's home for three years, telling no one, until the house was sold and she moved into an apartment near downtown Minneapolis. During that time, she wrote furiously, churning out volumes of short stories, reminiscences, and essays.

One day she phoned to let me know where she was and revealed she had been writing again. "It's pretty good, I think," she said, her voice vibrant.

She wanted to know how my writing was going. She had obtained a copy of my recent unauthorized biography of Garrison Keillor and had seen several of my articles in the *New York Times* before she returned to Minneapolis. "I could tell when you visited me at the office way back when that you'd do just fine in this world," she said. She pointed out that in the biography I had spelled someone's name differently three times on the same page. "Other than that, it was good," she said. Then she asked if I'd be willing to read some of her manuscripts and suggest marketing strategies.

"You were published in the *Atlantic* when you were seventeen," I said.

"That was long ago. Who'd remember? Can we meet for lunch downtown? I'd like you to read my stuff and tell me if it's any good."

I WAS STAGGERED by her bag-lady appearance. Her gray suit had stains down the front and hung on her. Though Jean was in her sixties, she could have easily passed for eighty. She needed a cane. Her face, highly rouged and caked with foundation, was haggard; her hair needed washing. She reeked of perfume and tobacco.

My cousin attacked her steak and French fries, which she washed down with a double martini. "I only drink on special occasions now," she said, smiling and looking at me, raising her glass.

As coffee was served, she opened the shopping bag at her feet and extracted manuscript pages—nearly three hundred in all—single-spaced and typed on a portable manual with a badly faded ribbon. Corrections written in pens of various colored inks or pencil were scrawled over the faint type of many pages.

"Read 'em and weep," she said, chuckling, and lighting a generic-brand cigarette.

I accepted the material, intending to look at it in the indefinite future. Three days later she called, asking for my opinion.

"I'm sorry. I haven't begun yet," I said. "I'll try to get started soon, though."

Her voice fell as she said she understood. "You have your work, I know. And you've heard me tell some of these stories anyway." Then she said there was no need to make her manuscripts a priority.

Over the next year I scanned a dozen stories from Jean's collection. Some were pieces built around her youth, often rages against her aunts. She had written a portrayal of her weak and inept father cowering before the termagants surrounding him. There was also an amusing reminiscence about a lunch with Bennett Cerf and Quentin Reynolds that had potential. Yet I put off calling her until I happened across a touching Christmas story. It was written from a young girl's point of view and dealt with the final Christmas before her parents' separation.

Finally I phoned and told her how much I liked the Christmas fiction. "Yes, it is a rather good story," she said. "What should I do with it? I was thinking maybe *Redbook*."

"Sure, why not?"

She said she had sent some stories to her son in Delaware. "I don't think he's much of a reader, but at least he'll know a little bit about his mother."

During the next several months I occasionally perused her remaining manuscripts. Several were well-written, trenchant observations of contemporary society, while others were reflections on the decisions she had made in life—leaving her child to pursue a career—and the emotional cost of those choices. After I finished reading everything, I called her. A male voice answered. It was Daniel with the news that his mother had died eleven days earlier. There had been no funeral service. He reported in an unemotional voice that apparently Jean, as he referred to her, had gone to the doctor a few months before with pain in her hip. It turned out to be cancer. The only person she told was her landlord. Cousin Jean spent her final months dying alone. The landlord informed Daniel of his mother's death after discovering his phone number on a desk blotter in Jean's apartment.

Daniel was still in Minneapolis cleaning out her rooms. "Unbelievable filth," he said irritably. "I'm tossing most of it into a dumpster. Talk about junk."

I offered to meet him the next day at his mother's place. It was nearly empty now, though thick particles of dust hung in the air. There were feline hairs on the carpet tinged with the odor of cat urine. We drank beer from cans and sat on a worn maroon sofa that would also go to the dumpster.

"How well did you know Jean?" Daniel asked.

"A little. We didn't get together often, but we talked on the phone from time to time. She'd been writing ever since she left New York."

He sighed. "Was she any good?"

"Sure. *Atlantic* published her when she was still in high school."

"Yeah, I know that." He lighted a cigarette and stared out the window at the dumpster in the street below.

After an uncomfortable lull in our conversation, I stood. It was time to leave.

"Was my mother a good person?" Daniel asked, not looking at me. After a pause he turned around. "I think you knew her better than I did."

"She was certainly her own person," I said.

UNCLE SEE-SEE'S SECRET?

THE FIFTY-YEAR MARRIAGE of my great-uncle See-See was our family's elephant in the living room. References to the marriage were infrequent, veiled, and never discussed. While See-See resided in my grandparents' tiny house for more than four decades, neither my father nor his eight siblings ever laid eyes on his wife, Maria, or saw a photo of her.

Everyone, including my grandfather, called him See-See, though his name was Pasquale. I'd been told as a boy that "see-see" was something of an Italian diminutive, an affectionate term referring to one's uncle. I learned years later that this wasn't authentic Italian but came from the dialect indigenous to the region of Calabria at the toe of Italy's boot—a mélange of Italian, Albanian, Greek, Saracen, Norman, and Spanish. My father's family pronounced the word for uncle, *zio*, as "see-oh" instead of the correct Italian "tsee-oh," and when referring to their Uncle Pasquale, shortened it to just the first syllable but saying it twice. When I said "Uncle See-See," I was, in effect, calling him "Uncle Uncle-uncle."

See-See was a man of few words, and though he died in 1946 when I was six, I distinctly recall his presence in my grandparents' kitchen. Each Sunday our large extended family would gather in the house at Duluth's western end for a ritual meal of antipasti, pastas, meatballs, sausages, and *dolce* (sweets) prepared by my *nonna*. The affairs were boisterous, with everyone gesturing, shouting, and laughing as food was passed and enjoyed.

But when the Fedo clan squeezed around the dining room *tavalo*, See-See chose seclusion in the kitchen. Toothless, with a brown poor-boy cap pulled low over his hairless head, he'd sit on a white wooden chair in the middle of the room beneath a bare lightbulb that descended from the ceiling on a cord. It was a scene reminiscent of Booth's *New Yorker* cartoons without the presence of demented dogs.

I retained a fondness for See-See, though I can't recall a single exchange of words between us. Perhaps my affection stemmed from the time he stopped my father from disciplining me for some boyish infraction. As Dad began to remove me from the kitchen, See-See hoisted his cane, menacing Dad, who acceded.

IN THE SUMMER OF 1904 three Fida brothers sailed from Naples to America, escaping the cruel poverty of Rosarno and all of Calabria. Uncle See-See, the eldest and only married brother, stayed behind. Giuseppe settled in Bridgeport, Connecticut, while Salvatore and Giovanni moved to Minnesota's Iron Range. Upon learning that two brothers had secured immediate employment in an Aurora, Minnesota, iron mine, Pasquale packed up his two oldest sons, Francesco, twelve, and Beniamino, eight, and joined them. See-See left Maria and their two-year-old son, Pasquale Jr., in Rosarno. Apparently the plan was for See-See and the boys to find jobs, send money home, and eventually save enough to bring Maria and Pasquale Jr. to America. None of the American Fedos ever brought up the subject of See-See's wife and third son until a decade ago.

A few months before his death, my father began to speak of his immigrant family. He disclosed that three of the four Fida (feeda) brothers received the name Fedo (fee-doh) from immigration minions at Ellis Island in 1904. In the course of saying he knew very little of their lives in Italy, or even much of it after their immigration, Dad broached the long-unmentionable issue regarding his uncle Pasquale.

A few years earlier, my brother David had discovered the existence of cousins back in Rosarno. I asked Dad about the connection. "They're See-See's people," Dad said and sat forward, his elbows on the kitchen table, large hands cupping his jaws. It was a pose he assumed during the later years of his life when he wanted to impart a story—a contrast from his aversion to them for most of his ninety years. We'd grown closer in the five years prior to his death, and now he found pleasure in sharing yarns about his growing up in Duluth's Little Italy neighborhood.

As he went on to resurrect old Pasquale, Dad said his uncle joined Giovanni and Salvatore in Minnesota but found life wasn't much better than in Rosarno, where Pasquale had been a cobbler. "I don't think he was a very good one," Dad said, "or he could have worked as a shoemaker here too. As far as I know, he never did." He and his boys eked out a hardscrabble existence for ten years, failing to save enough money to bring Maria and little Pasquale to America.

"See-See didn't talk much," Dad said. "So who knows what he thought about anything? He used to go off to work with Pa in the mornings, but did they work at the same place? Nobody asked, so nobody knew. Maybe he just took a streetcar downtown and sat around with the rest of the bums."

After a while Dad straightened up. "See-See gave me my first horn lessons, though. He used to be a decent musician, but how he ever afforded an instrument is beyond me. Give him credit for knowing music. He'd sometimes sing Verdi or Puccini if he thought nobody else was around."

Dad allowed that descendants of Pasquale Jr. were probably still living in or around Rosarno, but he had never bothered looking them up on his two junkets to Italy. "There wouldn't be anything to talk about," he said. "I can't remember my Italian, and it's not likely they know any English, so what's the point?"

I found the language barrier reference amusing. Italian neighbors in Duluth used to joke that during his forty-plus years in Minnesota, See-See mostly forgot his Calabrese Italian, while concomitantly he hadn't acquired much English, leaving him bereft of both languages.

My father chuckled at the recollection but sobered as he began to explain what I didn't know about See-See and the Calabrese cousins—*cugini,* Dad called them—and the ignominy that kept Dad and his siblings from visiting the Rosarnese *cugini.*

"After See-See had been here quite a while, years really, Beniamino was a problem. I guess today they'd call him a wise guy, like on *The Sopranos.* He was a punk, got into all kinds of trouble with the law. I remember going down to the jail with your grandmother, who'd bring him a bowl of spaghetti every Saturday when he was in the pokey. Anyway, he wasn't a citizen, so after maybe the fourth or fifth time he was arrested, they deported him." My father told me that while it pained Pasquale, it hurt my grandmother even more. She thought Beniamino could be salvaged if he stayed in her house, attended Mass at St. Peter's, where all Duluthians of Italian descent worshipped, and ate her homemade pastas and sausages.

But Beniamino was too far gone, Dad said, and it was assumed he preferred the criminal elements in Italy to facing prison time in Minnesota.

Some months after Beniamino's return to Rosarno, it was reported that he sent a letter to his father. When the young man arrived at his mother's home, he saw not only young Pasquale, now about thirteen years old, but also a seven-year-old little girl who called the lady of the house "Mama."

Furious, Pasquale terminated correspondence with Maria and ceased spousal support. The relationship was *finito*. Maria, however, persisted. In a passionate letter she wrote that in all the years of Pasquale's absence, he was a continual presence in her thoughts and dreams, some of which, she reported, were exceedingly vivid. In one of them he came to her bed and they made love. So vivid a dream, she said, had to be true. The little girl was the product of that dream, and on the Blessed Virgin, the child was Pasquale's.

The Calabrese were deeply superstitious, even while fervently embracing Catholic dogmas. My father's people attended daily mass but still harbored fears that someone might give them *il mal occhio*—the evil eye—which inevitably meant misfortune or suffering of some gravity. Perhaps a few early twentieth-century Rosarnese might have accepted Maria's explanation for the second Immaculate Conception, but not See-See. Though unschooled, See-See understood the improbability of such an occurrence and forbade the mention of Maria in his presence to the end of his days.

No one in the family ever heard of See-See's namesake again. However, I would learn that he died in 1969, still in Rosarno, a town despised by the American Fidas for the misery they endured. My grandfather Salvatore's bitter memories included foraging for food in dumps as a four-year-old orphan until at sixteen he volunteered for the Italian army, where he received dependable, though meager, meals and lodging. He considered his private's salary of ten cents per week as a bonus, from which he would purchase two packs of cigarettes, saving two cents for candy or other sundries.

Our family was never able to ask about his life in Calabria without him scowling and waving a dismissive hand. "Basta," he'd say. Enough. And the conversation, not quite begun, would terminate. I only knew his thoughts about the homeland because in 1959 he and I traveled to Detroit to visit his daughters and grandchildren—my aunts and cousins—and during the day while the adults were at work and the kids were in school, my grandfather and I were alone. We talked and he recalled Italy—Calabria—and the mean, impoverished life he left behind. But he never spoke of this in any detail to his own nine children.

The germ of my desire to connect with the family in Calabria likely was born during that long-ago visit with Salvatore, who upon arriving in America purged himself of his Italian name and was known in the new country as Sam.

I remained curious about what had happened to Beniamino, the "wise guy," as well as the illegitimate child of Maria and her unknown father. I thought maybe my father did too, but he died before my brothers and I would travel to Calabria in the summer of 2004.

Three years before we departed, David located the addresses of twenty Fidas in and around Rosarno. He wrote to all of them, wondering if any might be related to our great uncle. He received five replies, including one that began, "I Rosario Fida, deaf and dumb since birth, have nevertheless fathered 11 children." The prolific Rosario added he didn't know if we were related but would be pleased to have us visit.

Another respondent, Attilio Fida, indicated he was the grandson of our uncle Pasquale, and emphasized that Rosario was not. David maintained a sporadic exchange of letters until six months before our scheduled departure. His last two missives went unanswered, and we thought perhaps our cousin had passed away.

Meanwhile, David had also learned we had shirttail relatives who owned a tuna cannery in the fishing village of Pizzo. Since Pizzo was only twenty miles from Rosarno, and the existence of distant cousins was known, we decamped there, eager to inquire about the descendants of Pasquale. The Pizzo *cugini,* whose last name was Callipo, did not know the Rosarno Fidas. However, they shared a similar indiscretion with the Fidas, though they were less secretive about it. Giuseppina, the great-great-grandmother of the present tuna magnates, had been a consort to a baron during the worldwide depression of the 1890s. Her service brought both shame and survival to her family, as she was the only means of support, owing to the baron's generosity. Several years later the baron gave her the tuna cannery, which the Callipos have maintained for more than one hundred years.

THE CITY OF ROSARNO (with a population of 15,000), though situated on the coast of the Tyrrhenian Sea, is not noted for beaches or other diversions, and American tourists are almost unheard of. Recently the town has been beset with Mafia issues. Following years of persistent pressure by Sicilian *polizia,* the criminal enterprise expanded to Calabria. Moving across the Strait of Messina to Calabria seemed logical to Mafia dons because, as we learned from a Pizzo businessman, there were only two police officials in the entire region assigned to investigate organized crime. Franco, our bed-and-breakfast proprietor, argued we should not visit Rosarno, saying he would not be comfortable with our traveling there. But we could not be dissuaded.

We drove to the Rosarno Municipio, hoping to find out what happened to Attilio Fida and perhaps to discover other relatives in the region. Officials at the city hall were helpful despite language difficulties, and the deputy mayor said Attilio was not only alive but was a friend. He phoned, and our cousin hurried to meet his long-lost relatives and cart us off to his home. Through a translator, Attilio said he'd never received David's latest letters.

Within minutes of our arrival, food magically appeared, brought by other relatives who lived in the same middle-class neighborhood. Attilio's oldest brother, Fortunato, carried in several gallons of his homemade red wine. Long tables were set in the garden beneath trees heavy with ripening apricots. Nearly forty Fidas and Fedos sat down for a spontaneous welcome-home, get-acquainted feast.

See-See's grandchildren—Fortunato, Rocco, Attilio, Clara, Maria Rosa, and Maria, a nun stationed near Rome who was not at the reunion—ranged in age from sixty to seventy-three. None of them ever saw their grandfather. Yet he retains icon status among the Rosarno Fidas, and each of his grandsons named one of their sons after him. During the 1970s, there were three little Pasquale Fidas gamboling on the Via Nazionale, where the families live.

Upon learning that I was the only one present who had ever known old Pasquale, Fortunato and Maria Rosa wept and Maria Rosa produced photos dating to the 1870s: a five-year-old See-See with his mother—the first photo I had ever seen of my great-grandmother, another of him as a young man in an Italian army uniform, and finally as an adult shortly before his departure for America. In this latter he is erect, rangy, unlike the stooped and toothless old man of my memory. There is also a photo of a lovely Maria, she of the Immaculate Conception, at about age thirty. Maria Rosa pressed the photos of her grandparents to her breast, wept, and embraced me, moistening both sides of my face with her tears.

In this moment pungent with reunion and loss, I was unable to broach the subject of Maria's love child and whether her relations were included in this gathering.

We did learn that Beniamino became a "businessman" and served as an interpreter for Allied troops after the invasion of Italy. But the family never heard from him after 1950, learning only that he had died in Rome sometime during the 1960s. No one knew the manner of his death and seemed uncomfortable talking about him. Our cousins said he hadn't stayed long in Rosarno after he'd returned from America and were content to let the matter drop.

While thrilled to have met my long-lost relations, nagging questions remained after I left Rosarno. Who was Maria's daughter? Who was the child's father? My cousins must have wondered about their grandfather, why he never wrote or visited. That he might have abandoned Maria could be understood, but what about little Pasquale? Italians, so noted for family attachments, do not forsake their children or aged parents. There are very few if any nursing homes in Italy, and day care centers for children are also rare. It goes against the character of these people to not nurture children and to not care for the elderly. But my great-uncle left a wife and child without communication for the last thirty years of his life. Why would my cousins so revere such a man?

Still, the presence of the first Pasquale was palpable during our visit. Conversations were sprinkled with references to "Papa," who left for America never to return and who never, as far as I knew, wrote letters, sent money, or remembered birthdays after his alleged cuckolding.

Back home in the states, my brothers and I continued to receive occasional notes from cousin Attilio; in several he asked about the absence of communication from his first cousins—Pasquale's American grandchildren—whom David had phoned following our connection with the family in Rosarno. Attilio reported that he had written three letters to each cousin but had received no response. When my brother attempted to intervene on Attilio's behalf, he too was stonewalled.

Other American cousins tried recollecting comments about See-See that their parents had made years before. Several of my octogenarian aunts were asked about See-See and the story of his wife's infidelity. Responses varied; while all had heard the account, some doubted its veracity. From one came this oblique observation. "They used to say that See-See was something of a ladies' man."

Was this the answer? Was the infidelity See-See's rather than Maria's? If so, had See-See fathered an out-of-wedlock child?

I AM FOUR OR FIVE YEARS OLD, visiting at my grandparents' home. Two strangers are present. One is a woman with protruding dark moles on her face and neck; her thin, black mustache draws my attention until my mother nudges me and whispers that I must not stare. With her is a whiny, fat girl about my own age that the woman calls Sylvia. I am urged by other adults in the house to be nice to the girl and go outside to play with her. Fortunately, Sylvia throws a tantrum and refuses to join me. I spend the rest of the afternoon beneath Grandpa's apple tree, tossing its wind-fallen fruit at the abandoned chicken coop in the backyard. At dusk, Sylvia and the woman leave the house with Dad's bachelor brother Frank, get into my uncle's Pontiac, and head down the hill. Sylvia and the woman absent themselves from my mind. I never hear of them again, but in recent months I am haunted by their presence in my grandfather's house, and I think I recall seeing the woman gently fondling See-See's hand as he sat in his kitchen chair. Was this woman his daughter or daughter-in-law? Was the fat, unhappy Sylvia his granddaughter? Our family's allusive communication pattern persists, so my questions are met with shrugs or terse pronouncements such as "Who knows?" "Could be," or "Your guess is as good as mine." Other American relatives have no recollection of either Sylvia or the woman who accompanied her on that long-ago visit.

I have considered the notion that Maria Fida had become, in the parlance of those times, a "white widow"—a reference to wives abandoned by the thousands when their husbands left to find work in America or Australia. See-See may have chosen to forget Maria, an easy task, as no one in the family would ever make inquiries about her or Pasquale Jr.

Basta, as Salvatore used to say. Enough. That I am no closer to learning the whereabouts of a cousin who may or may not exist is something I'll live with, at least for now.

RADIO DAYS

I RECALL LISTENING with my mother to morning breakfast programs before I was old enough for school. There was *Breakfast in Hollywood,* with Tom Breneman, whose shtick was prowling the audience and trying on ladies' hats, to the great amusement of his studio audience and astoundingly to the radio listeners who could only imagine the portly gentleman donning women's hats. Mother always laughed when Breneman would say something like, "Well, ladies, how about this one?" Mother once told me that Breneman was fat, and four-year-old I rejoined, "He doesn't sound fat."

The other morning program we listened to was Don McNeil's *Breakfast Club,* out of Chicago. Its opening theme song still resonates nearly seventy years later: "Good morning breakfast clubbers, good morning to ya . . ." Floyd Holm, brother of Mother's friend Elizabeth Holm, sang with the Escorts and Betty on that program, along with two other Duluth natives, Ted Clare and Cliff Petersen, with whom Mother went to Central High School. Petersen eventually became producer of *The Breakfast Club* and sometimes appeared on the show as a rustic with a heavy Swedish accent. His son Tommy occasionally lived in Duluth with his grandparents and attended Grant Elementary School for a while. He was in my sixth-grade class.

Mother and I also listened to her favorite soap operas: *Old Ma Perkins, One Man's Family, Stella Dallas,* and *Mary Noble, Backstage Wife* are the ones I best remember.

I was, of course, much enamored of children's adventure programs like *The Lone Ranger, Sky King, Jack Armstrong,* and *The Green Hornet.* Later on I almost never missed the Saturday morning show *There's No School Today* with Big John and his elf partner, Sparky.

By the time I was in the ninth grade at Washington Junior High School, I'd begun listening to *Bob and Ray* on KDAL and loved their satires of boys' adventure shows and soap opera spoofs like "Jack Headstrong: All American American," "Matt Neffer, Boy Spot Welder," "The Lives and Loves of Linda Lovely," and "One Fella's Family," as well as their man-on-the-street interviews conducted by roving reporter Wally Ballou. "The highly regarded Wally Ballou," winner of sixteen diction awards, was performed by Bob Elliott. My delight with the work of Elliott and Ray Goulding continues to this day; I frequently listen to my four-CD set of some of their finest skits.

Over the years, Bob and Ray sometimes worked in persons of local renown, most notably Odin Ramsland, who was for many years the general manager of KDAL. His name might appear in a Wally Ballou interview. These pieces were gentle satire except for the time in the late 1950s when Ramsland pulled the plug on the CBS feed of *Bob and Ray.*

Rock-and-roll music was rapidly ascending, and teens and the younger demographic had become the sought-after radio market. Bob and Ray were broadcast at 4:00 p.m. on weekdays, about the time teens were getting home from school. Another Duluth station, WEBC, featured a Top 40 format and dominated afternoon ratings. Sadly, Bob and Ray were off the radar, and Ramsland wanted to compete with WEBC, so he notified CBS that he'd be dropping the award-winning and highly regarded comics.

On the last program that would air in Duluth, Wally Ballou picked out some yokel for an interview. The interviewee was quite a dullard, unable to answer questions coherently. At the conclusion of the bit, Ballou said something like, "Thank you for talking with me today, sir, and if you would please tell us your name and where you're from." The response was, "I'm Odin Ramsland from Duluth, Minnesota."

Though I wasn't there, I was told by friends who worked at KDAL that upon hearing Ramsland's name, the station's premises erupted with raucous laughter, and the announcer in the booth, who was supposed to give the station break ID, time, and temperature, sniggered all the way through the announcement.

DURING THE LATE 1950s I was contemplating a career in radio, and as a freshman at the University of Minnesota–Duluth I auditioned for a spot on the staff of the student-run, low-wattage AM station, KUMD. Although I landed a position, I never quite distinguished myself until decades later when I persuaded Twin Cities giant WCCO to give me a five-minute Sunday morning spot to talk about fitness and health. I was at that time the Midwest editor of *Runners World* magazine. I also did live radio coverage of the Twin Cities Marathon for its first two years. Much later, I read essays on Minnesota, Wisconsin, and Florida public radio. I never, however, achieved career status in broadcasting.

There were many risible instances at KUMD as tyro announcers frequently committed gaffes. Once our program director wanted a young announcer—I'll call him Milton Walcovoulevich—to change his name. Milt was a year ahead of me in school and was a KUMD engineer who noodled with the often-problematic transmitter. Milt wanted to be on the air as well, and the program director agreed to give him a twice-weekly shift. After Milton's first broadcast, the director said, "Milt, you might want to consider doing something about your name when you're on the air." Milt agreed.

The next time he opened his microphone, out came "Good afternoon. This is your host, Jim Walcovoulevich."

EVEN BEFORE THERE WAS a television station in town, in 1951 Dad purchased our neighborhood's first TV set—a 27-inch Kaye Halbert from Everett Kreiman's TV shop between Eleventh and Twelfth Avenues East on Ninth Street—and ours was the first family to watch snowy screens and test patterns from weak signals picked up from Twin Cities stations. I remained interested in radio. I suppose even as a kid I was drawn to imagination and the life of the mind that was inherent in audio-only presentations. I still am and find new delight each time I go online and find archived old-time radio shows like *Fibber McGee and Molly, Lux Radio Theater,* or *The Shadow.* As I listen to them now, I feel a sense of loss for my children and grandchildren who missed out on those creative, informative, and amusing radio days.

THE TREE

"THE TREE" WAS A COLUMN I cowrote with Mike Zempel for the Duluth Air National Guard's 179th Fighter Squadron monthly newsletter. It didn't begin as a column, nor was it our intention to turn a small notice of a car for sale into a journalistic feature. The squadron was undergoing its annual summer training at Volk Field near Wisconsin Dells during the last two weeks of July 1959. Mike and I had unhappily been assigned by the guard as personnel specialists. That might sound impressive, but our duties mostly consisted of filing and dispensing forms and, in our case, sometimes misfiling them. We certainly were not specialists and were frequently bored with our tasks.

One morning Mike and I decided to initiate a prank on Don Kallberg, a gentle, soft-spoken man who was the assistant administrator in the personnel office. We would put Don's car up for sale, well below market value. We typed a for-sale notice with Don's phone extension and tacked it to the squadron bulletin board outside the headquarters building.

But as we headed back to our office, a captain stopped us, saying the for-sale notice was not authorized. "The bulletin board is for military announcements only." We were ordered to remove it.

"Then where can we post this, sir?" I said.

The captain shrugged. "Not on the bulletin board."

Mike and I stood for a moment, looking for another spot to place the for-sale notice. Several yards from the bulletin board was an old oak tree, the breeze gently rustling its leaves. We tacked the notice to the tree and returned to the office.

Within minutes we observed passersby stopping to read the posting on the tree, while almost no one was reading the bulletin board.

Fifteen minutes later Don answered a call from a prospective buyer. But instead of telling the caller that there was a mistake, that someone was joking around, he calmly answered questions. "The tires are practically new," he said. "About 40,000 miles," he said. "No, it isn't air conditioned." Finally, "Well, I've decided not to sell it." When he hung up, Mike and I were limp from laughter.

Don said, "Did you guys put my car up for sale? I don't want to sell my car. What gave you that idea?"

Before we could respond, his phone rang again, and he once more politely answered inquiries, terminating this call with "I think I'm going to keep the car after all."

He fielded several more calls, then noticed a cluster of airmen before the tree. "Is that where my car is listed?" Don said. He marched outside and tore down the notice, returning and tossing it in a wastebasket. "What gave you the idea that I wanted to sell my car?"

"I think you said something about it the other night," Mike said.

"I did not, and even if I did, I wouldn't sell it for $900. It's worth at least twice that."

"We figured you would dicker with the buyer," I said.

"It's not for sale," Don said with finality, but he still had to deal with another half-dozen calls throughout the day.

Because of the notoriety of that announcement on the tree, Mike and I began writing whimsical and farcical articles to post. We hastily flitted through our official duties in order to spend time composing material for the tree. We justified ourselves with the argument that no one read military forms, but airmen clustered around the tree throughout the day.

Many of our readers weren't aware they were reading confabulations, like the time we printed a review of a nonexistent lecture in the chapel on Native American art and crafts by Sergeant Gil Sidney. We tabbed the event as must-see and that those who missed it last night should call the sergeant for information regarding this evening's presentation.

After answering many phone queries, an agitated Sergeant Sidney came to our office, chiding us not only for the prank but for doing it on duty time. The otherwise sweet-natured sergeant didn't threaten us with disciplinary action, or perhaps that hadn't come up yet in our conversation. He was interrupted by a major—the base chaplain—who told Gil how much he anticipated the 7:00 p.m. lecture and that he had invited several of his officer friends. We urged Gil to return to his room and brush up on his notes, since the chaplain would be in attendance. "I'll fix you guys," Gil said, exiting. But he never did, unless you count after he received a special commission as captain four months later, when he sought out Mike and me during one Saturday drill. While everyone else enjoyed morning and afternoon coffee breaks, he ordered us to stand at attention. Each time he dismissed us with a wide grin.

SOMETIMES WE CONSULTED *Bartlett's Quotations* and incorporated some into our articles and notices. Once, following a retirement party for a master sergeant, we ran a story laden with encomiums attributed to men in attendance but articulated by Francis Bacon, Jean Paul Sartre, T. S. Eliot, and Casey Stengel, among others. Due to the free-flowing intoxicants at the affair, only one of those present to whom we'd assigned a comment inquired. The quote we'd given Roger Facelli was from William Wycherly: "With faint praises, one another damn."

Facelli couldn't recall making that remark and asked what the hell it was all about. Nonplussed, Zempel responded. "Aw, Roger, you know how things go at these parties. It was probably just something offhand that you said."

Roger shook his head slightly but seemed to accept what Mike told him. "Okay, I guess," he said, wandering off.

Then there was the time we spliced together quotes that made no sense, ending with an altered quotation from Oliver Goldsmith: we changed "When lovely woman stoops to folly" to "When lowly airmen stoop to folly."

We posted that piece at the base of the tree, so everyone would have to bend down in order to read it. Observing from our nearby window, we were amused both by those who, following their reading, stood scratching their heads in confusion, as well as by those who got it and stood wearing sheepish grins.

One day our supervisor, Master Sergeant Jones, ordered us to stop writing for the tree and busy ourselves with refiling the squadron's morning reports. About 10:30 a.m. the commanding officer, a colonel, entered the office, which snapped to attention. Ignoring Sergeant Jones and everyone else, he stood before Mike and me. "At ease," he said. "Now, where is your story on that tree? I expect you'll have it up by noon chow." He pivoted and departed. Sergeant Jones glared at us. "Well, you heard the colonel."

Our columns were noticed by Captain Gordon Slovut, who was information officer with the guard and also a reporter for the *Duluth News Tribune* at the time. He would later become a health writer for the *Minneapolis Tribune*.

Following completion of the two weeks in Wisconsin, Slovut asked us to continue our column for the squadron's monthly newsletter under the heading "The Tree." The column virtually freed us from clerking. Whenever Jones told us to get busy with office duties, we always responded that we were under orders from Captain Slovut to write the next "Tree" column.

KEEP YOUR EYES OPEN

ON JULY 25, 1948, I was nine years old and mad for baseball. I played on age-appropriate baseball and softball teams, both based at the Central Field playground on Tenth Avenue East and Eleventh Street, about a block from our house. That morning I learned that the day before, the bus carrying the Duluth Dukes, a professional team in the class C Northern League, had collided with a truck that had crossed the center line on Highway 36 in Roseville, Minnesota. The team was on its way to a game in Eau Claire, Wisconsin. Five members of the Dukes, including the manager George "Red" Treadway, pitcher Don Schuchmann, infielder Steve Lazar, utility man Gil Tribl, and star centerfielder Gerald "Peanuts" Peterson, were killed in the crash. All the other players suffered season-ending or career-ending injuries, including third baseman Elmer Schoendienst, younger brother of Red, the St. Louis Cardinals star. Only four from that team would ever play again. Among those were Mel McGaha, who eventually made the big leagues as a coach and manager.

All my neighborhood chums had baseball heroes on the Dukes team. We listened to the play-by-play radio broadcasts by Bill Kirby on WDSM and pored over the box scores in the next day's *Duluth News Tribune*.

Peanuts Peterson, who batted left-handed like I did, was my favorite, and in 1947 he was voted the team's most popular player by Dukes fans. At the time I didn't realize it might have been because Peanuts was practically a local boy—a standout three-sport athlete from Proctor, a Duluth suburb.

We boys rooted mightily for our Dukes, cajoling parents into buying us their T-shirts and ball caps. The luckier among us might get a Dukes sweatshirt for his birthday.

One Saturday morning, my brother David and I took the East Eighth Street bus downtown where a couple of Dukes players were signing autographs and meeting fans at the Tri State Sports store on Superior Street.

Peanuts Peterson was supposed to be there, but he wasn't, and so David and I stood in line to have a pitcher, Joe Svetlick, sign our official Duluth Dukes scorecards. I was mildly disappointed, but I brightened when Svetlick picked up my scorecard and, mussing my hair with his hand, said, "Hey, how you doin', slugger?"

He gave me his signature and instantly became my favorite pitcher. But since I wasn't a pitcher, Peanuts remained my favorite everyday player.

ON THAT TRAGIC JULY MORNING we learned to our horror that the fatal, fiery crash had wiped out our Dukes. No survivor would be able to continue with the season. The parent club of the Dukes, the St. Louis Cardinals, cobbled up a squad from within the farm system, but they were players we didn't know and had never heard of, and as it turned out, the team didn't make the playoffs. I don't think I ever saw the faux Dukes play a game.

I don't recall any of our gang crying over the loss, but we were devastated. How could baseball players die like that?

"It probably happened so fast that they died before they could remember to keep their eyes open," Larry offered. None of our gang laughed at the comment because we believed it. Death meant closed eyelids; immortality beckoned, we reasoned, if when faced with death or serious illness, you persisted in keeping the eyelids wide apart. Still, we worried that something like that could also happen to us; we'd be dead before we could think to keep our eyes open.

I suppose my boyhood buddies and I couldn't have been more than six or seven years old when we began having serious discussions about mortality. All of us had been thinking about what would happen to us if one or both of our parents suddenly died. We knew parents of children died because there was an orphanage on Fifteenth Avenue East and Fifth Street, not far from our neighborhood, and most of us had seen the large three-story house.

It troubled us that it wasn't only old people who died. One boy in our crowd had a cousin who died when he was a baby. "He was too little to know he shouldn't close his eyes," the kid said.

"You won't die if you keep your eyes open," affirmed another boy. "You try as hard as you can to keep them open and you won't die."

"Why don't old people keep their eyes open?" said someone else. "My grandma died before I was born."

"I don't know. I bet old people like grandmas and grandpas probably just forget until it's too late."

We agreed we wouldn't forget when we got old. There would be no dying among our group.

But the subject didn't die, and every now and then it came up, though we always affirmed the necessity of keeping the eyes open, and if you somehow just couldn't do it yourself, you'd have a friend close by who would hold them open until you got well.

We strove to keep our minds off mortality by playing baseball or softball practically every summer day up at Central Field. But when the number of kids available didn't add up to a couple of teams, we'd play four or five on a side at the intersection of Tenth Avenue and Tenth Street, using the manhole cover for home plate. First base was the mailbox on the northwest corner of Tenth Street; second was a tar patch in the middle of the street, and third was a glove of someone from the team at bat, placed on the southwest curb on the avenue.

I hoped to be a centerfielder like Peanuts Peterson but was consigned to right field by the midget league team from Central Field in the Duluth playground league. Actually, I was delighted to be playing right field—usually considered the least desirable position in kid leagues because hardly anyone ever hit the ball to right field. But I was only nine years old, and the midget teams consisted of boys from twelve to fourteen. I should have been playing in the younger cadet league, but I was thought to be enough of a "slugger" by older boys so I played midget ball instead.

ONE DAY AT CENTRAL FIELD, Kenny's big sister overheard us discussing the eyes-open theory. She scoffed and said that was stupid.

Their grandmother had lived with them, and when she died her eyes were wide open. "Daddy had to close them," she said, and he kept them closed by putting pennies on them. Kenny said he had never heard that before, and I don't know if the rest of us believed her, but over the Labor Day weekend, Marlowe, one of my teammates, drowned in Pike Lake just outside of town. Keeping your eyes open wouldn't help if your lungs filled with water. He had just turned fourteen and was a splendid ballplayer; his last-inning homerun had won us the city championship only a few weeks before.

SHORTLY AFTER the U.S. involvement in the Korean War began, we would realize that people we actually knew, who were not old, could and did die.

There were a couple of high school guys who had hung around Central Field for several years. They were stars for the David Wisted American Legion Post team that held practice sessions there. My own baseball aspirations consisted of one day being good enough to make the Wisted team and lead the league in batting.

American Legion teams were composed of sixteen- to eighteen-year-old boys. One of these was Bernie Walczak, who hung out with his friend, another Peanuts, after workouts. Often Bernie and Peanuts would solicit boys our age to shag fly balls as they pitched to each other for extra batting practice. I was always happy to perform this service because Bernie, who didn't know my name, used to call me "Slugger," as Joe Svetlick had done.

Once in a while, after Bernie and Peanuts had finished their routines, Bernie would tell me to grab a bat and he'd toss me a few pitches. Peanuts didn't linger for my at bats; Bernie was more dedicated to baseball and actually played professionally for the Dukes a couple of years later.

About the time we noticed that we hadn't seen Peanuts around Central Field for a while, we learned he had been killed in action during the first weeks of the Korean War. By then we knew keeping your eyes open would not thwart the grim reaper. It was now beyond discussing; we were ten- and eleven-year-olds, and as worldly-wise as boys our age could be.

BERNIE GERL, THE ALL-STAR Dukes catcher in 1948, spent forty days in a hospital recovering from his injuries. Two years later he was able to return to baseball, spending time with teams in Houston, Texas, and Montgomery, Alabama. In 1952 he returned to the Dukes, playing two more seasons there before retiring. Still a decent player at the mid–minor league level, his injuries deprived him of his power stroke with the bat. Gerl would be the last surviving member of the 1948 Dukes, and he returned to the old ballpark a couple of years ago to toss out a ceremonial first pitch in a summer league for college players. He reminisced with aging fans and talked about the crash that may have kept him from reaching the big leagues.

He had a tough road to recovery in 1948, but as everyone in our kid gang back then would have said, he kept his eyes open and survived, and after leaving baseball, he became a commissioner of the park district in his hometown, Joliet, Illinois.

BASEBALL DAYS

I WAS A GOOD ENOUGH baseball player in my youth to get a tryout with the Duluth Dukes in 1957. At that time the Dukes played in the Class C Northern League as a farm team of the Chicago White Sox. I don't think the Dukes management thought I might actually make the team, but they probably figured it was a good public relations gesture to occasionally extend a one-day look-see to a local kid.

I batted left-handed, and I was not without credentials: co-captain of the Central High School team during my senior year and a batting average of .400 for two straight seasons. Although I had trouble hitting curveballs from southpaw pitchers, I faced lefties only once or twice a season, and I thought with more exposure, I'd learn to hit them nearly as well as I did right-handed pitchers. My other weakness was throwing. I showed minimal arm strength and accuracy from my favorite position, third base, and in high school and American Legion competition, our first baseman, Dave Baker, snatched my sometimes errant throws, keeping errors to a minimum.

But all this is hindsight. At the time I thought I might impress the team enough to at least send me to class D, perhaps in Holden, Nebraska, where I might hone my skills and be promoted to the Dukes in a year or two.

While my hitting would usually top our high school and legion teams, my most noteworthy diamond achievement occurred in a midget league game (teams with boys aged twelve to fourteen) when I made an unassisted double play from right field. It drew attention because outfielders seldom if ever get that opportunity. In actuality, it wasn't all that remarkable. With a runner on first base, the batter hit a soft fly ball to shallow right field. At the crack of the bat, the runner took off for second. I dashed in and caught the ball just beyond the infield grass and noticed the runner was nearly at second base. I continued running, beating him by a stride back to first for the double play.

On the bench our coach chastised me for not throwing the ball to the first baseman, who was calling for it, and the runner would have been out by several yards. "You wanted to be a big shot, hey?" he said.

I guess I did.

DURING THE LATE 1950S, White Sox teams were built around speed and defense. They didn't hit many homeruns but bunted, stole bases, slapped the ball around, had good pitching, and won a lot of games.

When I arrived at Wade Stadium, Dukes manager Joe Hauser greeted me. Hauser had enjoyed several decent major league seasons, but was better known as a minor league slugger who hit sixty-nine homeruns for the Minneapolis Millers in 1933.

Hauser was accompanied by another former big-league player, now a White Sox scout, Johnny Mostil, who had been the only major league center fielder ever to catch a fly ball in foul territory.

Both men were old-time baseball lifers, now in their late fifties or early sixties. They had me run a half dozen wind sprints, then put me out in left center field to shag fly balls. Each man had two baseballs. Mostil struck the first one toward the left field foul line. "Get after it, son," he hollered, and I did, grabbing it on the fourth or fifth bounce. As I was throwing it back toward him, Hauser smacked another toward dead center field. "Whatcha' waitin' for?" Mostil shouted. "After it, sonny." The men repeated this regimen over and over, each hitting a ball well beyond my reach and urging me to "get after it."

An eternity of agony. Within minutes I tasted blood and my lungs burned. Then Mostil hit one back toward the scoreboard and on rubbery legs I began another chase. I saw and felt the cinder warning track before the wall, but coordination vanished and I could not stop or even muster strength to raise my arms for protection against the inevitable, imminent collision.

Crumpled on the ground, wounded and gasping, I heard Mostil's voice. "You gotta get those if you want to play in the big leagues, son."

End of tryout and professional baseball dreams.

WELL, NOT QUITE. During the 1962 Northern League season, the Dukes were affiliated with the Detroit Tigers. My friend Bill Jacott was departing Duluth for medical school and recommended I take on his old role as public address announcer for the Dukes. It would be an ideal job since I was completing my undergraduate degree at the University of Minnesota–Duluth during the summer sessions, and except for weekends, all games were played at night.

Al "Moose" Lakeman, another former big-league player, was managing the Dukes. A mountain of a man, who stood over six feet tall and must have weighed about 250 pounds then, Lakeman had been a backup catcher throughout his career. During the season he lived at the Lincoln Hotel on Third Avenue West and Second Street. The ball park, Wade Stadium, was at Thirty-fourth Avenue West and Grand Avenue, more than two miles distant. Lakeman didn't have a car during his Duluth stay and would walk from his hotel to the stadium and back again.

Occasionally he'd accept my offer after games to drive him to his hotel on the condition that we stop on the way at the Pickwick, his favorite Duluth watering hole, and let him buy me beers. He had a prodigious capacity for steins of the locally brewed Fitger's and wanted me to keep up with him—a hopeless task. Moose could down a stein in a single swallow, while I was a nurser, which tried his patience. Within minutes, he'd have emptied four steins while I was still working my first, with three more fresh ones on the table before me. "Come on," he'd cajole. "You're way behind, boy."

He'd let me off the hook when I'd insist I had to drive, and he'd quickly down my untouched beakers before we'd depart.

He once told me his favorite season as a player came not in the major leagues but in Milwaukee, during its Triple-A American Association days. One opening day, Moose hit a ninth-inning homerun to win the game for the Brewers. A local *Braumeister* rewarded him with a case of free beer every week for the entire season.

While Lakeman's Dukes didn't win the 1962 pennant, several from that team went on to play for the 1968 World Series champion Detroit Tigers. Willie Horton, Jim Northrup, and Mickey Stanley were with the 1962 Dukes and major contributors to the Tigers' success.

AS PUBLIC ADDRESS ANNOUNCER, I sat alone in a booth in the last row of the grandstand directly behind home plate. On rare occasions, I'd get a visitor—usually a member of the Dukes board of directors during games when a cold wind was blowing. While the booth was unheated, it did provide a barrier against chilly breezes coming in off Lake Superior. But there was one semiregular visitor—the bus driver for the Sioux Falls Canaries team.

He was an affable man with stereotypical truck-driver heft, perhaps six feet tall and packing about 225 pounds. The Canaries visited Duluth several times that season, and without fail, the driver would watch the games with me in the booth. I always enjoyed the badinage with the man I knew as John and looked forward to our Sioux Falls series more than any other because of him.

We both enjoyed baseball, but our discussions were far-reaching; we jibed about politics—me Democrat, John Republican—and movies and music. He was a big country music fan, who thought the sun rose and set on Johnny Cash.

Northern League home teams usually played a Sunday doubleheader, and on the Canaries' second trip to Duluth the teams played two games that Sunday. Sioux Falls took the first one, and the young man who pitched that game joined his driver and me in the booth to watch the second game. At one point, John left to get a hot dog and soft drink, and the pitcher and I continued chatting. I told him I really liked talking to John during the games.

"Who's John?" the pitcher said.

"Your bus driver."

"Ah, so that's Bussy's name." (Bussy was and is a generic name for drivers of minor league teams.)

John returned, and if memory serves, Sioux Falls won the second game as well, giving both John and the pitcher a good-natured chuckle at the Dukes' futility that day.

On the final Canaries' trip to Duluth in late August, after the final out of the last game, I told John how much I'd enjoyed his company. I asked what he'd be doing once baseball ended, and he said he'd be resuming his normal Greyhound route, Sioux Falls to St. Paul. He stood, ready to leave, and held out his hand. "It's been fun knowing you, Mike," he said, nodding, but his forehead furrowed and his lips pulled downward. "There's one other thing," he went on. "My name's not John. It's Ben. I wouldn't have minded if you were the only one calling me John. But now guys on the team and lots of other folks think that's my name too."

JOE DIMAGGIO TURNS HIS LONELY EYES TOWARD THE GIRL AT 2833 WEST THIRD STREET

A WHILE BACK I joined an old Duluth Central High School baseball teammate for lunch. Now a retired entrepreneur, he said that he spends a month each summer traveling around the country watching minor league baseball games in places like Schaumburg, Illinois; New Britain, Connecticut; and Albuquerque, New Mexico. "Even Brooklyn has a minor league team now," he told me. "It's not Ebbetts Field, but it's great to see baseball in Brooklyn again."

Then he mentioned how much he had enjoyed playing our high school tournaments at Wade Municipal Stadium, home of the Northern League Duluth Dukes, adding, "You know, that old Duluth ballpark is still as nice as any I've seen."

I told him that a long time ago Joe DiMaggio said the same thing.

IN 1937 after completing his second season as star centerfielder for the New York Yankees, twenty-three-year-old Joe DiMaggio was offered a cameo role in a Hollywood movie. The money was easy, and he wouldn't have to go to California; the film would be shot on location in the Bronx.

On that same sound stage, a nineteen-year-old beauty from Duluth, Minnesota, was cast in a nonspeaking part as a nightclub dancer. The movie was the long-forgotten *Manhattan Merry-Go-Round*. But the girl, born Dorothy Arnoldine Olson, now known as Dorothy Arnold, met the baseball star on that set, and both of their lives were changed. Only months earlier, Dorothy had boarded a train for Hollywood, where she hoped her sapphire-blue eyes, striking good looks, and modicum of musical talent would get her noticed by entertainment moguls.

Dorothy appeared in a dozen or so films at Universal Studios over the next two years, including *Secrets of a Nurse, House of Fear, Pirates of the Skies,* and *Phantom Creeps.*

Her career was bit parts and walk-ons and would never advance much beyond these. She didn't need a press agent until she became linked with the Yankee Clipper and her name and photo appeared in all the gossip columns. In July 1939 they announced their engagement on the day before the Major League All-Star Game. In addition to her large diamond, Joltin' Joe promised Dorothy a homerun in the game and, in storybook fashion, delivered. DiMaggio went on to record his highest-ever batting average that year—.381—which won him the first of two consecutive American League batting titles. The engagement caused a lot of excitement in Duluth, and it was hoped that the batting champion would visit the city, perhaps after the World Series ended.

Was it possible, locals wondered, for the wedding to be held here? After all, aren't most weddings performed in the bride's home church? What was Dorothy Olson's church anyway?

Could out-of-the-way Duluth host the wedding of Joe DiMaggio? The national press would be attending and hosts of sports and show business figures. The most ardent of Chamber of Commerce boosters realized our city likely would not be considered for such an occasion, even given that the bride was a favorite daughter. If Dorothy had been from one of the Twin Cities at least the state could have basked in the spotlight of celebrity nuptials.

Finally, as everyone expected, when the wedding took place the following November it was in DiMaggio's San Francisco hometown at Saints Peter and Paul Catholic Church. In the largest wedding ever in that city, more than twenty thousand people jammed the streets around the church, causing the entire bridal party to be late for the ceremony.

DiMaggio's only visit to Duluth occurred during the week of January 11, 1941. Dorothy's father, E. A. Olson, was a railroad conductor, and the family lived in a working-class neighborhood at 2833 West Third Street. The house is a modest two-story wood structure, as are most of the homes in what has become a neighborhood of retirees and younger families in varying degrees of financial stress. DiMaggio himself came from working-class stock; his father and brothers were fishermen. And while the Yankee icon was one of baseball's genuine superstars, he wasn't that far removed from his days as a high school dropout on the streets of San Francisco's Little Italy where most immigrant families struggled with daily living expenses as they did in Duluth's West End.

The Olsons lived barely one mile from where my father grew up, and Dad must have passed the house hundreds of times on his way to Denfeld Senior High. It would never have occurred to him that "the great DiMaggio" (as Santiago called him in Ernest Hemingway's *The Old Man and the Sea*) would in any way be connected to this rather drab neighborhood.

And he wasn't really, spending only five days in Duluth during the dead of winter. Local politicians and well-heeled sports aficionados feted him at the downtown Athletic Club. He was taken to the site of the nearly completed Municipal Stadium, home of the Class C Northern League Duluth Dukes. According to a story in the *Duluth News Tribune*, "Joe DiMaggio trained a pair of critical eyes on the fences at Duluth's new ball park yesterday, dug his heels in a snowdrift at home plate, and glanced at the left field foul pole 340 feet distant. Doffing his homburg, DiMaggio swung at an imaginary pitch and said, 'Baby, batting out a homer in this park will be a good job for the best of 'em.'" Then he accompanied Duluth's mayor and ballpark architects on a march around the grounds, making suggestions for improvements that could be in place by the start of the 1941 season.

When a columnist asked DiMaggio how he liked his wife's hometown, he replied diplomatically, "I like Duluth from what I've seen of it."

Fearing crowds, he wouldn't see much. The paper reported that he was recognized only once, when he entered a flower shop to buy roses for his wife. A customer merely asked if he was Joe DiMaggio and timidly requested an autograph.

Later that day DiMaggio was to try his hand at curling at the Duluth Curling Club rink. Whether or not he hefted a broom and swished it as he shuffled along the ice attempting to guide the curling stone toward its target never made the papers, but his quotes about wanting to see his wife skate did. He did not skate himself, nor did he don skis, telling the *News Tribune* that having been raised in California he had never tried winter sports, and if he did so now, he'd expect a wire from the Yankee front office ordering him to stop any activity that could put him at risk of injury.

In all he appeared in a half dozen *News Tribune* photos during his stay, mostly grinning with his wife and her family or posing with Duluth dignitaries around a banquet table. Unlike later stories of his aloof nature, he seemed friendly to local residents who glimpsed him, and he joked easily with the press.

I do not remember DiMaggio's visit to Duluth, but I distinctly recall my second birthday the following May. I am sitting on the living room floor upstairs in the Lakeside neighborhood duplex on Regent Street, where my mother, father, and I lived. My father is kneeling several feet from me, holding a baseball bat and ball. I am wearing a regulation-size fielder's glove on my left hand. It is his birthday present to me. Dad lightly taps the ball with the bat, and it rolls slowly over the faded mauve carpet, stopping when it bumps my glove. "Atta boy, get the ball," he shouts. He retrieves the ball and bunts maybe three or four more rollers my way before laughing and hoisting me onto his shoulders, telling my aunts and uncles and grandparents that I'd be another Joe DiMaggio one day.

IN THE DECADES following this visit, dozens, if not hundreds, of Duluthians who lived far from 2833 West Third Street claimed to have seen DiMaggio wandering about that neighborhood, purchasing a carton of Chesterfield cigarettes in a drugstore, enjoying a chocolate sundae at Bridgeman's, even helping one stranded motorist push his car from a snowbank.

Duluthians were thrilled with DiMaggio's presence here and wished him well for the 1941 season, in which he would set his fabled fifty-six-game hitting streak and win the Most Valuable Player award over Ted Williams, who set an equally significant mark that year batting .406, the last time a major leaguer has hit .400.

The city had embraced DiMaggio almost as one of its own ever since his engagement to Dorothy, and residents hoped her film career might blossom from the steady publicity she received with her husband. There was also speculation about the genetic talents their children might inherit.

But this marriage was never stable. Joe was an inattentive yet very jealous husband. They had a son, Joe Jr., in 1941, but neither Dorothy nor Joe Sr. spent much time parenting the boy. Joe liked to have his wife travel with him, though he often left her in hotels while he spent evenings with cronies.

Dorothy left him in the middle of the 1942 season, and Joe slumped; the Yankees pressed her to return. At season's end, however, she filed for a Reno, Nevada, divorce. At Joe's pleading, she withdrew her petition. Many thought he wanted to save the marriage to avoid the military draft, but when that hit the papers, he had to enlist to avoid being labeled a coward. A year and a half later, while her husband was in uniform, Dorothy split again, calling Joe cruel and indifferent.

At their 1944 divorce hearing, Dorothy claimed that Joe demanded she be subservient to his career and abandon her own. She agreed to this, with unhappy results. Joe, she charged, provided a home, but he was never in it. By the time the divorce was final, DiMaggio's staunchly Roman Catholic mother was looking after Joe Jr. and continued to do so, having in a way disowned both her son and Dorothy for separating. Though he failed to appear in court for the proceedings, Joe was hurt by the dissolution, and until he met Marilyn Monroe in 1951, he never gave up hope of reconciliation.

In fact, he believed he and Dorothy would remarry after the 1946 season, but during spring training she married a stockbroker named George Schuster. This union didn't last even as long as her marriage with Joe, and in 1949, she divorced again. She later married a man named Ralph Peck, and together they owned and operated a Palm Springs nightclub, Charcoal Charley's.

Dorothy Olson began her career as a youngster singing with the Duluth Salvation Army band. She appeared in local children's revues and sang with a dance orchestra during her summer breaks from school.

According to Dorothy's sister, Joyce Hadley, a talent scout saw Dorothy sing in clubs and thought she should go to Hollywood. She would later take two screen tests with Paramount before landing a contract with Universal Studios. Despite the feeling in Duluth following her divorce from DiMaggio that she had given up a promising film future to be a full-time wife and mother, the truth was that in Hollywood, she was just another pretty face with only modest talent, easily replaced for roles calling for lovelies to sit at restaurant and nightclub tables, stroll by in department stores, or lounge on beaches. A day's work here and there, broken by phoning agents and casting directors, followed by weeks of waiting for return calls.

Her name resurfaced in America's press after Joe and Marilyn became an item, and Marilyn seemed especially close to Joe Jr. Dorothy went to court, seeking an increase in child support (though the boy had lived mostly with Mama DiMaggio) and also to ask the judge to prevent Joe Sr. and Marilyn from taking the boy to public places "where there's drinking and jive talking."

She lost on both counts, and the judge chided her for divorcing DiMaggio in the first place. From then on, Dorothy was out of the public's eye, having failed to rejuvenate her film career, making only one more appearance in a 1957 flop titled *Lizzie*.

Though her third marriage lasted until her death, it apparently was a rocky relationship, and despite her 1952 plea that her son not be exposed to public drinking, Dorothy herself took to the sauce.

A former entertainer at Charcoal Charley's remembered our Dorothy as beautiful to the end of her days. He recalled that often after she'd had a few gin Gibsons, she'd get up and belt out Broadway show tunes for patrons at the club. She was also something of a raconteur, spinning anecdotes about Walter Winchell, Humphrey Bogart, Lauren Bacall, Dorothy Kilgallen, Elsa Maxwell, Adela Rogers St. John, and Anita Loos.

Dorothy died of pancreatic cancer in 1984 at age sixty-six, after seeking nontraditional treatment for the disease in Mexico. Her son, following a dissipated life that included homelessness and chemical abuse, died of a drug overdose six months after Joe Sr.'s death in 1999. Today Dorothy Arnold is little remembered in Duluth, except among a few octogenarians who recall a pretty young girl singing her heart out in the Denfeld High School auditorium, a girl surely with a golden future, a girl who was reaching for but never quite grasped the world on a string.

JOGGING WITH
JAMES JOYCE

THE NOVELS OF JAMES JOYCE had always loomed monstrously impenetrable to me during my undergraduate years as a literature student at the University of Minnesota–Duluth. I had never considered this a handicap, but it does heighten the rather absurd circumstance in which I found myself one damp Dublin morning.

It was our first afternoon in the city, and my wife and I had stopped at Neary's Pub, a favored haunt among the Dublin literati. "Yeats used to come here," I told Judy. "And the whole Abbey Theatre crowd."

We entered as a burly bald man was arguing the merits of James Joyce as the world's foremost novelist. As we were seated, he stared at me and thundered, "No man who calls himself literate sets foot in Dublin without he pays his respects to Mr. James Joyce."

The barb stung, for in certain circles back home, I was considered very well read indeed. Still, I had never managed to read all of *Ulysses* and consequently failed the midterm exam in English 220-something-or-other at the University of Minnesota–Duluth.

So when this man who introduced himself as Yancy DeSilva, an exiled poet from Idaho, asked if we would accompany him to Sandycove, the area of Joyce's last Dublin residence, I felt moved to acquiesce.

In 1904 Joyce and another writer, Oliver St. John Gogarty, shared a Martello tower for a time, and the tower has been turned into a small Joyce museum that would doubtless interest those enraptured by Joycean prose.

Sandycove itself is a decent stretch of beach, familiar as the opening scene from the film adaptation of *Ulysses*.

"What that tortured genius had to endure here," said DeSilva, possibly attempting a parallel with his own semisqualid state.

"Gunfire forced him to leave, you know," he continued. "Samuel Tench, who was staying here temporarily, had recurring nightmares that used to wake everybody. So Gogarty, whom we later know as Buck Mulligan in the book, got frustrated. One night he fired a gun to scare Tench. But Joyce panicked and split instead."

My lack of enthusiasm caused DeSilva to stalk out of the tower, and on the bus back to town he remained sullen. However, upon arriving, he requested we adjourn to Neary's again. Judy begged off and went to our guesthouse.

DeSilva and I were seated at a table with some students from Trinity College, and DeSilva quickly steered the conversation to Joyce. During the next hour, quaffing countless Guinnesses and porters, he suggested that we run the route Leopold Bloom took on his odyssey through the novel. I mentioned it would be quicker than reading the book.

One of the students, Burt Costello, said he was a fan of Joyce, a veteran of road races, and would be happy to escort us and point out spots of interest along the way.

It didn't seem like a bad idea. I had been jogging three miles five days per week at a leisurely pace for several years back home. I had run the Park Point five-mile race, and I was anticipating entering Grandma's Marathon the next year.

However, after nearly four weeks of junketing about Europe, my body was succumbing to the sweet temporary trimmings of the fat life—cognac and Camembert, layers of rich double cream over fruit flans. Now there was noticeable shortness of breath when I climbed castle stairs or joined walking tours. And neither of us realized that the course, taken in order of the text, might well extend over ten miles.

We agreed the run would start at Eccles Street at 9:30 on Friday morning. According to Joyce, Bloom lived there and began his day fantasizing about grilled mutton kidneys and other organ meats.

At the top of Eccles Street the morning air stank of overflowing garbage cans and the sidewalks were littered with bottles and scraps of paper. A dozen or so kids were caterwauling in the street where Burt Costello limbered up with calisthenics. "Right on time," he greeted.

A battered pickup truck pulled over to the curb, and DeSilva rolled out and sat on the curb holding his head in his hands. The driver, a thin, reedy man, helped him remove his coat and shirt. DeSilva was otherwise clad in a pair of worn gabardine trousers and sandals. He spit on his hands.

"Might as well get started," Burt said.

Slowly. Eccles Street is a short street, and we took it easily. DeSilva hung about ten yards behind Burt and me, snorting and clearing his throat. We stepped into Dorset Street and crossed it. "George's Church," Burt called, pointing.

DeSilva fell farther behind, cursing loudly as we hit Temple Street, then Parnell down to O'Connell Street, the main artery of downtown Dublin. Across the River Liffey along Sir John Rogerson's Quay, we slip into open spaces amid street buskers moving up to O'Connell Street. I feel a clutch in my throat; sweat stings my eyes.

Burt seems pushing for a six-minute-per-mile pace. My lungs burn. He heads onto Westland Row. "Oscar Wilde was born here at number 21," he shouts.

Propelling myself toward Burt and pulling even, I gasp and ask how much farther.

"A couple miles on there's Sandymount. Bloom headed for the funeral up that way." Then he was off again along Fenian Street to Bath Avenue, maintaining a narrative of sorts that eluded me, as did the novel.

Finally he slowed, breathing easily, while my legs were turning to jelly. A knot stiffened in my left calf. "You don't seem to be holding out here," he teased. "Come on then, we'll head on back to the center of things."

He again hollered out streets as we passed by, and we recrossed the River Liffey. DeSilva was leaning over the bridge. He turned and rubbed his eyes as we ran by. "Aaargh," he spat angrily and turned again over the water.

Up once more to O'Connell Street. Then turning onto Henry Street to Moore, a vendor offered me a peach, the crone matching me stride for stride and screaming, "Nine pence—no, for you only eight." Calling on all the reserve I could muster, I managed to leave her after twenty yards. Across Abbey Street then back across the river to Bachelor's Walk and finally down Grafton Street. Joyce and DeSilva had become blurred. My brain a puddle, my stomach contracting violently, I stopped as Burt ran on, and I lost him as he turned a corner.

A momentary swoon, and I steadied myself against a parking meter. Burt had come back looking for me, and I stumbled into him on Duke Street. He helped me along, and we stopped in front of Davy Byrne's Moral Pub.

The race was over. Joyce and DeSilva could disappear, and yes, I couldn't care less.

Burt said then that he didn't think I could make it. Yes, I agreed, but it was all right. I hadn't really finished the book either.

And yes, right in the middle of the sidewalk, I sat down. Burt hoisted me to my feet, and he asked me, will I quit now, yes, and perhaps stop in for a pint? Yes, to quench my thirst; yes, to take a load off my legs; yes, and to forget Joyce. Yes and yes, my heart was going like mad, and yes, I said, yes, I will, yes.

AT THE FLAME

THE DULUTH RESTAURANT of legend and lore in my boyhood was the Flame. During its more than four-decade existence, it had three locations in town, most famously the last one, on the bayside waterfront at the bottom of Fifth Avenue West. It was the city's premier supper club with live music in addition to a pricey menu. For a number of years, a turbaned waiter known as "The Sultan of the Second Cup" poured customers' coffee.

Diners sometimes boarded the S.S. *Flame*, a cruise boat anchored alongside the restaurant, which would take passengers on tours of the Duluth–Superior harbor. These were especially popular on languid summer evenings; from the lake, passengers could view the lighted city on a hill. Neither the restaurant nor the cruise fell within the Fedo budget, but it was the place to which most of my friends and I aspired. I made it for the first time at a fraternity brother's wedding reception, and later as an entertainer with my performing partner, Dan Kossoff.

While the club didn't headline celebrity artists, there were times when wealthy Duluthians celebrating birthdays or anniversaries rented the facility for events and imported marquee names like comedian Alan King.

Usually the club featured dance orchestras with female vocalists in the main dining room, while the downstairs lounge offered smaller combos or, most of the time, a cocktail pianist doubling on vocals. For several years in the mid- to late 1950s, the lounge was home to an engaging piano player, Billy Samuels.

Samuels was born in Mississippi but moved to Chicago, where he formed Bill Samuels and the Cats 'n Jammer Three during the 1940s. The group had a hit record in 1947 with the novelty tune

"Open the Door, Richard," and Bill's version of "I Cover the Water-front" also landed on some charts. He wasn't the vocalist on "Open the Door, Richard," but during his Flame tenure he often treated customers to the Johnny Green waterfront ballad and also performed some good old shouts and blues pieces during late-night sets. Samuels was a popular staple in the Twin Ports during his Flame tenure, which ended when he moved to Minneapolis in the early 1960s and died there at the too-young age of fifty-three.

ONE TUESDAY MORNING in August 1963, while Dan and I were between gigs (primarily because Dan was finishing his degree at the University of Minnesota in Minneapolis), I received a call from Charlie Kasmir, the Flame's personable major domo. Club owner Jimmy Oreck had fired his lounge pianist the night before and needed an immediate replacement for the rest of the week. Charlie heard that Dan and I had worked clubs and coffeehouses throughout the Midwest and wondered if we were available to fill the void. He didn't mention salary, and I didn't ask. We'd only performed twice in our hometown—at St. Scholastica College and a Snow Week show at the University of Minnesota–Duluth. But this was the Flame, the most prestigious supper club in town, and they wanted us.

I told Charlie I had to call Dan in Minneapolis but would get right back to him.

"Make it snappy," Charlie said. "Jimmy wants to see you at two this afternoon."

It was about 10:00 a.m. when I phoned Dan and said we might have a job at the Flame, but Jimmy Oreck wanted to see us with our guitars at two o'clock this afternoon.

"I'll jump in the shower and head right up," Dan said.

WE ARRIVED AT THE FLAME several minutes early, and Charlie said Jimmy would need to hear us, so we should get ready. If he liked us, we were hired. Charlie ushered us to a cluttered room the size of a large closet. It held extra bar stools, coatracks, rolls of toilet paper, and sundry other detritus. We cleared space for our guitars and tuned up, then went back to Oreck's office. We could hear him from outside on the phone, barking at a vendor about a requisition. We'd heard Oreck was prickly and irritable; we didn't know what to expect.

Finally he beckoned us with his hand to enter his office. He did not speak and remained seated behind his desk, where he immediately swiveled away to stare out the window at Lake Superior. "Play," he ordered.

Dan and I glanced at each other, shrugged, and launched into our standard first set opening song, Blind Blake's "Run, Come See Jerusalem." But during the first verse, Oreck abruptly stood and left the office. Assuming he'd only momentarily stepped out, we finished the number and then waited about five minutes before packing our instruments. Discouraged, we were about to leave when Oreck appeared in the doorway. "Be ready at seven," he snapped. Then he disappeared.

"Did he even hear us?" I said.

"Who cares?" Dan said. "We got the job."

On opening night, the lounge was about half-filled. Steve, the portly, jovial black doorman, was our biggest fan. Turned out he knew more than a few of our songs—Leadbelly pieces in particular—and sang along with us from his doorway station.

On Wednesday, our second night, we invited Steve to sing along a couple times, but at 10:00 p.m. the restaurant hostess told us not to do that anymore because "Jimmy doesn't like it."

Thursday night Jimmy ducked into the lounge, shook his head at the sparse gathering and said, "We're not making a dime here."

According to waitresses, Oreck was a crabby perfectionist who often berated them. One night after a set I ordered a chicken salad sandwich. The server paused for a moment. "Wait until after nine," she said. "Jimmy will be gone then, and it'll be on the house."

At the week's end, Friday and Saturday nights drew standing-room-only audiences. One of the waitresses told us on Saturday that the crowd was larger downstairs than up. "Been a long time since that's happened," she added.

That final Saturday, a local doctor and his wife hired us for a private party, offering $150 for an hour of songs and comedy. Oreck had us split $250 for our five nights and wasn't there when we closed.

Charlie Kasmir gave us a check and bought us a drink, but we never heard a word from Mr. Oreck.

Regardless of Oreck, in the aftermath of the Flame engagement, I felt ascendancy as a performer, expecting other significant gigs to follow. But our entertainment career would only last through November. Despite our resumé—the Padded Cell in Minneapolis, Omaha's Crooked Ear, numerous other coffeehouse and campus appearances—we were to discover that without a hit record, or even a recording contract, we'd gone as far as we could as entertainers. And while the money was decent for that time, employment was sporadic, and we both opted for lives of regular wages and benefits.

I NEVER VISITED the Flame again but learned that it struggled in later years, and the building was sold in 1978. It continued as a restaurant under several different names until it was demolished in 1998 to make room for the Great Lakes Aquarium.

A friend's father said Oreck contributed to the landmark's demise at least in part because he treated investors with the same disdain he did employees. "Once when he was in trouble, I loaned him money, and so did a bunch of other businessmen in town. We all thought the city should have a place like the Flame where you could entertain clients. Once I called for a last-minute reservation, and he tells me they're full. I mean, a couple weeks before, I handed him $5,000 because he's in trouble, and now he can't find me a table?" The fellow sighed. "Jimmy was like that with everybody. And it's a shame because that place should have gone on a lot longer."

Perhaps, but nightclubs with hatcheck gals and scantily clad cigarette girls—frequent settings in scores of noir films—were all succumbing, as Americans increasingly stayed home, enjoying free entertainment on television, where they could watch show business icons. Performers in clubs were held to the elevated standard of the greats, which they couldn't match. For example, Dan and I.

The passing of many fine-dining enterprises signaled the end of the era when an evening at a classy downtown supper club was far from commonplace. It was, for most of us back then, always a night to remember.

FOR A MOMENT DYLAN
PLAYED IN OUR SHADOW

WITH MY PARTNER, Dan Kossoff, I enjoyed a brief but heady run as a folksinger during the early 1960s. We played throughout the Midwest, appeared on numerous college campuses, and marqueed at the old Padded Cell in Minneapolis and the Crooked Ear, a coffeehouse in Omaha.

But while I was earning up to $75 per night in those early days, another native of Duluth, Bob Dylan, was picking up mere pocket change. Using his family name, Zimmerman, he played in coffeehouses in a neighborhood called Dinkytown near the University of Minnesota. At the time, we didn't pay much attention. We had our own ambitions.

In July 1963, Dan and I had played for a standing-room-only crowd at the Flame supper club in Duluth. Giddy with our success there, and warmed by solid reviews, we pondered our future success. We didn't know it then, but our show business careers would last only through November.

The ascent of rock 'n' roll was signaling the demise of the folk music bistros and coffeehouses. Dan and I had gone about as far as we could without a hit record—or at least a recording contract.

Meanwhile, Bob Dylan was on a rapid rise to icon status. Shortly after he took New York by storm, all of us back on the local folk scene were abuzz about the Minnesota kid who hadn't seemed all that impressive to us.

FOR DAN AND ME, the final months on the folk circuit proved a mixed bag. We certainly didn't please everyone who heard us.

One night the owner of a St. Paul coffeehouse called us over between sets. "I can't stand this," he said, grabbing our guitars. He cranked the tuning pegs on both instruments (not subtle adjustments, either), and handed them back. "That oughta do it," he said. Chagrined, I bought a pitch pipe.

Later we returned to Duluth to headline a concert at the University of Minnesota–Duluth. Unlike the St. Paul coffeehouse gig, this performance had gone well. Afterward, Dan and I went to a party at his in-laws' home.

I recall chatting with a pleasant middle-aged woman who seemed intrigued that we had just completed a show at the college. She mentioned that her son was also a musician. I merely acknowledged her comment and moved on. Later, I asked Dan who she was.

"That's Bob Dylan's mother," he said.

In one of our last performances, we were scheduled to play at the Padded Cell. It was the week of John F. Kennedy's assassination on November 22, 1963. The night after his death we agonized over which songs to play and whether we should use humor. The place was packed, but the crowd seemed reluctant to enjoy themselves.

The most memorable moment that night was joining Denver musician Walt Conley and Native American singer–actor Floyd Red Crow Westerman on stage for a lengthy rendition of "This Land Is Your Land." It may seem maudlin now, but at the time it was profoundly moving for us—and the audience.

A short time later Dan and I stopped performing to enroll in graduate school—Dan to the University of Kansas, Kent State for me—ending my short-lived show business career.

It was just as well. I was never much of a musician, and in an increasingly sophisticated music environment, my fingers couldn't manage fretting the guitar for complex chords like flatted fifths. My singing was mediocre at best. These days it's mostly limited to songs like "When You Wish upon a Star," shopworn lullabies, or Sesame Street novelty tunes to help my young grandchildren go to sleep.

Despite Bob Dylan's decades-long success, I sometimes wonder if he sings to his grandkids too, sending them off to dreamland with choruses of "Desolation Row" or "Subterranean Homesick Blues."

CHRISTMAS WITH THE KLINES

I SPENT MY twenty-second Christmas in a quiet hotel dining room in overcast downtown Omaha, Nebraska, while my parents and brothers celebrated at home in frigid Duluth, Minnesota.

This was my first Christmas away from my family and its holiday traditions. There was the selection on December 24 of a tree at Stan Darling's Pure Oil station, where Dad annually enjoyed choosing some bony old spruce nobody else wanted. Stan would sell it for a quarter because it was Christmas Eve. That evening we could anticipate the inevitable lutefisk and potato sausage supper at Grandma Norquist's house next door, accompanied by smothering hugs and kisses from great-aunts that left me redolent of their Youth Dew or Tabu. I'd miss the wild and noisy unwrapping of presents, followed by our pastor's midnight sermon at Bethel Baptist, which seldom failed to induce somnolence.

I was in Omaha as one-half of a folk singing duo. My partner, Dan, and I had accepted a two-week engagement at a coffeehouse called the Crooked Ear. We were fresh from our first gig at the old Padded Cell on Lake Street in Minneapolis, where we opened the night after the departure of an up-and-coming trio called Peter, Paul, and Mary. Dan and I hoped to emulate that group's success and felt it was in the best interest of our fledgling show business careers to take the Omaha job.

This meant, however, we'd be absent from our homes during the holidays, which was no big deal for Dan, who was Jewish and thus eschewed both the religious and commercial trappings of Christmas. I thought it would be no big deal for me either.

Opening night in Omaha was December 18, and we learned then that instead of the anticipated three sets per night, typical of a

bar gig, we were to play four or sometimes five sets, concluding anywhere between 2:00 and 5:00 a.m., depending on how many patrons
were still around. If there were more than five, we performed.
The first three nights the proprietor kept us working until 4:30
a.m., singing "Matilda" and "Scarlet Ribbons" to grumpy stockyard
workers who ventured in for morning cups of coffee before starting
their shifts. After postperformance meals, we returned to our midtown hotel and tried to sleep. We rarely saw daylight. Around 4:00
each afternoon, we'd leave the hotel, eat breakfast, and arrive at the
club by 7:00. Thus did our time pass in days of subfreezing, darkened
gloom. No way to spend Christmas.

Somehow word circulated that a Jewish folksinger was headlining at a downtown club, and by our fourth night the city's Jews
were flocking to see us perform. Not just kids either. Ladies in their
seventies, wearing jewelry and furs, and men in smartly tailored
suits sipped cappuccino alongside the flower children in their Levis
and sandals.

They roared with approval, no matter what we played. They
especially loved our Hebrew medley of "Tzena, Tzena" and "Artza
Alinu," which stopped the show while the audience demanded
encores.

Dan and I were taken in by these strangers, who brought us
to their homes for meals, feeding us lox and cream cheese on
bagels, chicken soup with fist-sized matzo balls, and great briskets
of beef.

Christmas Eve arrived, differing slightly from previous days.
We didn't begin until 10:00 p.m., by which time college students
had excused themselves from their families and headed downtown.
The Crooked Ear was packed that night, mostly with our Jewish
friends.

Just before we opened our midnight set with a rousing version
of Blind Blake's "Run, Come See Jerusalem," I felt the inexorable tug
of nostalgia. I suddenly craved the fragrance of balsam boughs that
always decorated Bethel Baptist's sanctuary and the scent of hot wax
from lighted candles placed in every stained glass window. "Bring
Me Little Water, Sylvie" played well to the crowd, but "Good King
Wenceslas" rang in my head.

Our new fans must have sensed my displacement, because a man and his wife, old enough to be my parents, stopped by after the set and invited Dan and me to dinner the next afternoon.

Mr. and Mrs. Kline met us in our hotel lobby on Christmas Day and drove us to another hotel and a dining room nearly void of diners, save three tables occupied by perhaps a dozen people we'd met during the past week.

"Mazel tov," they greeted, hoisting glasses of tea or wine as we entered,.

The room was filled with white-flocked Scotch pines, huge gold and blue balls, white lights and candles. "Got a table right here," Mr. Kline said, ushering me toward a seat where a miniature decorated tree stood on a placemat. "We call these things Hanukah bushes." He smiled. "You probably call them something else."

Wine was brought to the table and poured. Raising his glass, Mr. Kline turned toward me. "L'chaim," he said.

We all clinked glasses. Then food—glorious food, such as might have graced the holiday table of Charles Dickens himself—arrived, accompanied by bustling waiters. I tasted my first roast goose, with prune-and-apricot stuffing, mashed potatoes and gravy, sweet yams, cloverleaf buns, spiced apples, pumpkin pie, and coffee. And there was conversation—animated talk of politics, rock 'n' roll, and ethnic food.

By the time the Klines returned us to our hotel, darkness had descended over Omaha. Twinkling colored lights, strung on pine boughs over the downtown streets, bespoke the bonhomie of the season.

I don't remember many specifics of our shows that evening; I suppose they went well enough.

In the months that followed, there were more club engagements, but Dan and I seemed not cast in the molds of show business legends, and we gave our last performance during the week of President Kennedy's assassination in November 1963. Dan went on to become a producer for PBS, and I became a college teacher and writer.

Formal education and age have enhanced my happy-go-melancholy personality, and to many acquaintances I'm something of a cynic. Except for Christmas. Then I still get soft around the edges. Home is definitely the place to be over the holidays, home with family and friends and traditions.

Yet that long-ago Yuletide in Omaha is evergreen. I can't celebrate Christmas without thinking of "the kindness of strangers," to quote Tennessee Williams—the Omaha Jews who befriended me more than thirty years ago.

Amid the merriment of this holiday season there will be exchanges of season's greetings, of "Merry Christmas" and "Happy New Year." To these I add another, in fond remembrance of my friends in Omaha: *Mazel tov.*

REMEMBERING SATCHMO

DURING THE CENTENNIAL YEAR (2001) of the great jazz trumpeter, Louis Armstrong, there were numerous homages to the legendary artist by musicians who knew him and younger performers who felt his influence, as well as paeans from critics. Fans bought reissued CDs of his greatest hits. New Satchmo biographies were in the works.

Armstrong, who died in 1971, was a larger-than-life musician and performer. But he was also a warm human being.

I met the illustrious jazz musician back in 1953, when I was fourteen and Louie Armstrong and his All-Stars were headlining the annual Home Show at the Duluth National Guard Armory. Our Washington Junior High School band director encouraged his students to attend. I think he said something about giving extra credit to kids who showed him ticket stubs from the show.

I was a drummer in the band and also a reporter for the school paper. After arranging to attend the show with two friends, I thought I might try to wrangle an interview with Armstrong and write a feature for the next edition of the *Bugle.*

We went to the Sunday matinee and watched Satchmo sing and dance with Vilma Middleton, the All-Star's rotund female vocalist. Armstrong mugged; he blew his horn, and after about seventy-five minutes, he concluded the set with a foot-stomping rendition of "When the Saints Go Marching In."

My friends raced to get in a line for free ice-cream bars, but I wandered over to the backstage entrance. While two security guards joked with a vendor, I slipped between them and maneuvered down the hall, jostled by roadies and a juggler's scantily clad female assistants who were frantically looking for props. Finally I stood before the sparsely furnished dressing room used by the conductor of the Duluth Symphony Orchestra during concerts.

The door was open, and Armstrong was alone inside, seated behind a large metal desk poring over newspaper reviews of the film *The Glenn Miller Story,* in which he played a featured role. He was wearing a checkered bathrobe and slippers. A colorful tam covered his head, and a towel was wrapped about his neck. Reading glasses rested on the tip of his nose. Amid the chaos of crews and other performers, Satchmo was calmly scissoring articles from the papers, then pasting them in a large black scrapbook.

Nervous, I stood near the doorway, half-expecting to be evicted. Satchmo, concentrating on his newspapers, didn't notice me. Too timid to speak, I was about to slink away, when a middle-aged man carrying a fresh bundle of papers appeared and suddenly asked, "You waiting to see the boss, young fella?"

I nodded.

"Sure, come on in. He'll see you."

I followed the aide as he plopped newspapers on the desk. He stepped back. "Got a young man here wants an autograph."

Armstrong looked up. "Yeah, I'll sign for you, Buddy," he said, his voice a familiar low, gravelly rumble.

Though I really wanted to interview Satchmo, I thrust my notebook across the desk. He scrawled his signature on the first page, then paused. On the top of that page, I'd earlier written, "An interview with Louie Armstrong."

He returned the notebook. "What paper you with?"

I swallowed, then mumbled, "*Bugle,* a school paper."

He smiled and leaned back in his chair. "Is it a good paper, Buddy?" I later read that Armstrong called everyone "Pops," but during the next ten or fifteen minutes he referred to me as "Buddy."

"It's okay, I guess," I replied.

"If you're a good writer, it should be better than okay," he said. "Now what do you want to know?"

I had no idea. I'd never interviewed anyone before, let alone a celebrity. Finally I blurted, "How long have you been playing the trumpet?"

He told me he'd started as a young boy in New Orleans. I asked if he liked traveling all over the world. "I get to meet my fans, which is important in this business." Then he asked if I played a musical instrument.

I told him I was a drummer in the school band.

"You practice every day, Buddy?"

"Not always."

"Writing for the paper takes a lot of time, hey?"

"I guess so."

"Gotta have good newspaper reporters too. That's an important job." He inquired about the subjects I was taking in school and told me to work hard and do well. He said he was glad I stopped by to visit, because he always enjoyed meeting gentlemen of the press.

At the conclusion of my interview, we shook hands. "You be sure and send me a copy of your story now, Buddy," he said. "I've got lots of scrapbooks to fill."

Then he resumed his clipping and pasting, this soft-spoken icon, looking for all the world like anybody's grandfather.

But I never did send him a copy of the interview because the *Bugle*'s adviser refused to print it, saying an interview with a "jazz" musician had no place in our school's paper.

More than one hundred years after Louis Armstrong's birth, many notable musicians and writers recall his monstrous musical talents and his superb showmanship. But I remember Satchmo sitting in that dingy armory dressing room, a soft-spoken, gentle man who called me Buddy and who took time to show kindness and generosity to an awkward fourteen-year-old boy.

BROXIE

WHEN BROXIE FRANCIS MAIZ decided to become a psychology major at the University of Minnesota–Duluth in the fall of 1957, he was already thirty-seven years old and had never even set foot inside a high school classroom. Though I was only eighteen, and our backgrounds were vastly dissimilar, we became friends. A Southern black man, he endured a hardscrabble childhood, quite unlike my own. I had never known want and had enjoyed academic as well as athletic success in school.

I was a broadcasting student and thought it would be my destiny to become the next incarnation of Edward R. Murrow or maybe Arthur Godfrey.

In pursuit of my goal, I responded to a poster announcing a meeting of those students interested in working as volunteer announcers for the college's low-wattage AM campus radio station. We assembled in the station's basement studio, housed in a renovated custodian's storeroom.

A dozen aspiring announcers slouched in sagging, lumpy, garage-sale sofas, nervously smoking cigarettes and eyeballing the competition. Broxie was reading a copy of *Down Beat* magazine. Unlike the rest of us, he was stylishly dressed, wearing a tailored navy suit, white shirt, and dark tie. He kept a close-clipped mustache and Vandyke beard.

I straddled the arm of a sofa and sat next to him. He lowered his magazine and nodded at me. "Hey, how you doin'?" We shook hands and exchanged names.

Then the station manager, a Korean War vet wearing a faded fatigue jacket with staff sergeant's chevrons, stood and said that during our auditions we would be taped reading one minute of news before introducing a musical selection. Those of us who showed promise would be contacted within the week.

Broxie so impressed the management, however, that following his audition he was immediately given his own program. He was scheduled three nights each week from 8:00 to 9:00 p.m., hosting what would be an erudite show called *B. F. on Jazz.*

I too was deemed acceptable for announcing, and a week later was reading formatted openings to transcriptions from the Amsterdam Symphony Orchestra and other prerecorded programs such as *Talking about Health* and *This Is Your Army.* So much for Edward R. Murrow or Arthur Godfrey.

Broxie, born for broadcasting, exuded a graceful nonchalance while on the air. He shared intimate stories with listeners. He sounded like a favorite uncle imparting humor and wisdom to the family around the dinner table.

He quickly became a darling among bright, young faculty intellectuals, who'd sometimes gather in the studio during *B. F. on Jazz* and then take him out for a drink after he'd signed off.

On the other hand, my on-the-air personality was tense and immature. Except for accurately reciting the time and temperature, my ad libs were awkward and forced.

I used to compliment Broxie and tell him how much I admired his showmanship and ease, while complaining that I seemed unable to develop the poise and polish that came so naturally to him.

One afternoon Broxie sat me down and said that because I respected Arthur Godfrey, he thought I'd be interested to know what the Old Redhead said about how a successful broadcaster behaves behind the microphone. Godfrey had been a little-known Washington, D.C., disc jockey until he narrated President Franklin Roosevelt's funeral for a national radio audience on CBS. Resisting the stuffy formality of his peers, Godfrey wept as the cortege passed him, and millions of Americans were moved. That broadcast provided his springboard to prominence.

Godfrey was able to apply a broadcasting philosophy he'd been contemplating for months. According to Godfrey, Broxie reported, most announcers sounded stentorian, like formally dressed men in starched collars. "Arthur Godfrey's philosophy is that the announcer should be a companionable old friend over for a chat," Broxie said. "Just be yourself, man."

Then Broxie invited me to join him in the announcer's booth during that evening's *B. F. on Jazz.*

After Broxie's opening theme faded, he began the show with a story about Thelonius Monk. Broxie's voice was low, mellow; his cadences poetic, a spoken-word equivalent of Monk's best-known song, "'Round Midnight." Moreover, Broxie seemed to resonate to the artist's pain and rage. Finally, he played some Monk but not "'Round Midnight," which he said was too familiar and not really Monk's best.

Broxie asked his audience to listen to the language of jazz, to hear the gossip and the truth, and to learn to discern the difference. "There are lots of phonies making music," he said. "Just as there are lots of phonies in business or education or religion. It takes time, but it's important to expose the phony. He doesn't tell the truth."

He extemporized a short biography of Charlie "Bird" Parker and incorporated Bird's best-known quote about how vital it was for an artist to connect with, to *be* his work. "If you don't live it," Parker had said, "it won't come out of your horn."

Broxie played several more selections before his program ended. As he gathered up his long-playing albums and a few notes, he said, "You dig any of this?"

"A little, maybe," I said.

He grinned. "Take your time. Learn things. Watch people. Listen a lot. Read. Become wise." He paused. "You dig? Become wise." Then he asked me for a ride home.

It was the first of many rides I'd give him during the next four months. He didn't own a car and, surprisingly, didn't know how to drive. Broxie often requested ferrying for groceries, dental appointments, or to check out books at the downtown Duluth public library.

He was an omnivorous reader, devouring the volumes of black poets Langston Hughes and Countee Cullen. He also liked philosophy and biography.

Whenever I chauffeured, he would recount anecdotes about his life, his jazz acquaintances, and prominent prizefighters he knew from his own long-ago experiences.

He told me he left Alabama and the brutality of alcoholic parents when he was thirteen and made his way to New Orleans where he landed a job shining shoes in a Bourbon Street saloon. He talked of sleeping in a bus depot, cadging nickels and dimes from travelers. Broxie also became familiar with jazz in New Orleans, though it wasn't the traditional music for which the city is noted.

One afternoon a musician with the Count Basie band was in the saloon and Broxie gave him a shine. The musician told Broxie to go to the club where the band was playing that night, and he could meet the Count.

This introduction led to a two-year association with Basie. Broxie became a roadie, setting the stage before performances and striking the bandstand after the shows.

During Broxie's tenure with Basie, the Count presented him to many other jazz legends. Thus, when Broxie told his radio audience about Thelonious Monk or Mahalia Jackson, he was talking about people he knew.

One late November he asked me to drive him to a jazz concert in Minneapolis. We headed backstage after the performance, and I met another of Broxie's buddies, blind singer Al Hibbler.

Tape recorder at the ready, Broxie interviewed the artist who recorded the megahit "Unchained Melody" and scores of other jazz and pop tunes. The interview would be the centerpiece of the next *B. F. on Jazz* program.

Broxie and Hibbler discussed Billy Eckstine and Sarah Vaughan at great length because they were important crossover black artists whose influences were felt in both jazz and popular music. Suddenly Hibbler waved his hand and said, "They're great, but let me tell you who the best vocalists are today, the ones I dig and learn from. Frank Sinatra and Margaret Whiting. They know how to interpret a song. And with Frank nobody—*nobody*—is better with lyrics. When he sings, you know what the song means. A great singer pays attention to lyrics and diction. Singing is more than the notes."

I drove Broxie to other concerts and performances by lesser luminaries, and he, in turn, invited me to meet the musicians. These were people who had risen above poverty, lack of formal education, and racism. Their observations about the music scene and life were often harsh but sometimes sweet. One gap-toothed sideman of eighty said that every day with his drums was a joy and a blessing. Unfortunately none of these exchanges equipped me with the finesse required to succeed in radio. I remained stiff and unimaginative on the air. It wasn't for lack of effort, though. I spent so much time attempting to perfect my delivery that my grades suffered. With the draft board breathing down my neck, I joined the Air National Guard and was sent to San Antonio for training.

I'd promised Broxie I'd write and I sent him a letter every few weeks. He occasionally answered in one- or two-paragraph notes scrawled on lined notebook paper. He was reading Immanuel Kant, he told me in one missive, but thought the philosopher would be a bit weighty for me. "When you decide wisdom is cool, read him," he wrote.

About three months later I received a cryptic message in which Broxie said he had quit his popular program and had withdrawn from college. "Things change," he wrote. "Life isn't static. Time to move on. You were a friend. Be wise. B. F."

I wrote him the next day, but my letter came back stamped: "Return to Sender. No Forwarding Address." I would never hear from Broxie again.

In the subsequent decades I've gone long stretches without thinking about him. I never landed a job in broadcasting, unless you count the year I spent as a part-time gofer at a Duluth TV station after I returned to college, or the summer I worked as the public address announcer for a minor league baseball team. But several weeks ago I received a questionnaire from the alumni association from the university where I'd attended graduate school, requesting a few paragraphs on a person who profoundly influenced me during my student years. My submission would be included in a booklet of impressions of favorite teachers by "graduates of our institution who have made noteworthy contributions."

I wrote about Broxie and divulged an anecdote I had shared with him. As a ninth-grade reporter for the Washington Junior High School *Bugle*, I interviewed Louis Armstrong between sets at the Duluth Home Show in a grungy National Guard Armory dressing room. My Satchmo article was rejected by the paper's adviser, who said a story about a *jazz* musician had no place in a school publication. "Don't be too hard on the lady, Michael," Broxie responded. "Where she came from jazz was gutter music that didn't belong in polite society. Who knows—maybe she sees it differently today. Folks can change. Give them the benefit of that possibility." I wrote that Broxie, absent of baccalaureate and graduate degrees, had significantly impacted my intellectual development. I looked forward to reading the published volume.

As a writer, I'm used to dealing with rejection, but I was disappointed by the note turning down my brief essay about Broxie. "We found it interesting," wrote the editor. "However, we were looking for reminiscences about *professors* who have influenced students. Unfortunately Mr. Maiz was not a teacher and does not meet our criteria for inclusion."

BROTHERHOOD WEEK
IN DULUTH

THOUGH ONLY THREE YEARS OLD IN 1943, I was aware of World War II because my father's youngest brother Joe was a marine PFC in the South Pacific. In my mother's old scrapbook there's a snapshot of me engulfed beneath his overseas cap and looking at a saber he'd removed from the body of a Japanese fighter on some tiny atoll.

Because of Uncle Joe, family discussions of the war centered on Japan as the enemy, with more oaths directed toward Hirohito and Tojo than Hitler. My father's Italian family was ashamed of Mussolini—Il Duce—and sometimes felt embarrassed by their ethnic names. My aunts, I later learned, endured slurs at work or on the street—wop, guinea, dago—and privately the family prayed for Italy's capitulation.

But my most enduring impression of the war was taken from a poster I saw in front of the Apostolic church on the corner of Tenth Avenue East and Sixth Street in Duluth. It must have been in 1943 or 1944. I could not yet read. Mother was pushing baby brother David in a stroller, and we were walking down the hill past the church. I don't know the content of the poster's printed message, but its visual remains.

Jesus had thrown a stiff right cross into the face of a caricatured buck-toothed, slant-eyed Japanese soldier. A plethora of stars surrounded the hapless soldier's head; his face was contorted into a painful grimace. His helmet was separated from his head by the force of the Godly fist. The poster pleased me because I knew my uncle's job was to kill Japs. That's what we called the enemy then, not Japanese, and so did the radio commentators I heard each morning while eating Cheerioats (later renamed Cheerios) with Mother in our kitchen.

IT IS LATER THAT SUMMER and we are riding the Grand Avenue bus in downtown Duluth. Mother is holding David on her lap. The bus is taking us west on Superior Street toward the home of one of Mother's friends where we are to be lunch guests.

Suddenly traffic stops amid sirens and the flashing lights of an ambulance and police cars. From my window seat on the bus, now in the heart of Duluth's bowery, about Fifth Avenue West, I see a dark-skinned man lying face up on the sidewalk in front of a saloon. The man is wearing a blue work shirt and overalls, and blood is pooling beneath his head.

Several feet away, other men are restraining a pale, balding man wearing a powder-blue T-shirt, who struggles to escape and briefly does so before police grab him and shove him into a squad car. Mother, clearly distressed, urges me to not look out the window; she is calming David, who has, for some reason, begun to wail. But I remain riveted on the tableau, the shards of violence. Finally we are moving again, and I ask Mother if the man on the sidewalk is dead.

No, she doesn't think so. But she asks if I would like her to tell me a story. David isn't crying now, and she pulls me toward her, directing my gaze from the window.

But I have been transfixed by what I've just seen and the images won't clear my brain—indeed, sixty years later they still haven't. A bleeding man on the sidewalk, and another man, much lighter-skinned, has obviously caused him serious injury, but how?

I interrupt Mother with questions about the man police arrested, about the victim, about why nobody stopped the fight. She has no answers, and her tense, worried face says she wishes to God I'd not seen any of this.

We arrive at her friend's house, and I immediately launch into my child's eyewitness account of the incident before Mother shushes me and urges me to go to another room and play with toys.

I remember nothing of the rest of the day until we arrive back home during the late afternoon and Mother brings in the evening *Duluth Herald,* which has covered the bowery fracas. Mother discovers answers to some of the questions I'd earlier posed.

"The men were drinking alcohol," she says, screwing up her face. In Mother's Swedish family, liquor in any form was a scourge, and we'd do well to avoid it. But she summarized the newspaper story for me. The man police arrested said he hated Indians, so he went outside and knocked an Indian man unconscious. The victim had been taken to St. Mary's Hospital where he was treated and released.

"Do we hate Indians too?" I said, looking up at my mother from the scattering of toy building blocks on the floor of our living room.

I have no memory of her reply.

ON SATURDAY MORNINGS during my fourth- and fifth-grade years, my friends and I attended the weekly serial movies at the Lyceum Theater downtown. We viewed a variety of westerns with Red Ryder and Eddie Dean, but our favorites were the Charlie Chan mysteries, where we saw, for the first time, portrayals of stereotypical minorities. While the Oriental Charlie Chan was imperturbable, inscrutable, we always cheered when Mr. Chan's black chauffer, Birmingham Brown, played by Mantan Moreland, appeared. Birmingham Brown was superstitious and easily frightened, but his comic exchanges with another black rustic—Benjamin—delighted us. Birmingham would greet his friend, "Hey, the last time I saw you—."

"Not him. I run off that old hound dog—."

"That new suit looked real good so when he—."

"Then she fell in the creek, and—."

"Yassuh, but his wife never did catch that chicken."

"Oh, thass right, but then he had this hat see—."

"You ain't never seen a fat lady dance like that."

And so on.

In later years I would be haunted by the screen image of Birmingham Brown, his round face, his large terrified eyes as he stood alone in the dark trying to screw up courage against ghosts or spirits or loud noises. What must the black kids have thought of Birmingham Brown? Or Stepin Fetchit? A least Charlie Chan was brainy. Birmingham Brown was a numbskull—a comical stereotype featured for the amusement of white audiences.

But on the schoolyard we used to engage in Birmingham Brown patois with each other, those fractured conversations that went nowhere yet tickled us as we emulated Birmingham and his crony. I never thought of how this seemingly harmless nonsense affected the few black children who attended U. S. Grant Elementary School in Duluth on Eighth Avenue East and Tenth Street. Even though Grant was located in a middle- to lower-middle-class neighborhood, there were only a handful of black kids there—all of them from either the Bean or Potter families, except Archilee Fox, a very pretty sixth-grade girl, who just one year later would leave school to marry an airman stationed at the local air force base. There was George Bean, who was always called Bo, and his older sister Florence. The Potters were a much larger clan, but I was only familiar with John, Bernice, and Otis.

John, a year ahead of me, was from about the fourth grade on the best natural athlete in the school. He was always the strongest, fastest kid in his class.

His younger sister, Bernice, however, was the largest person in our fifth-grade class and also the strongest. She topped one hundred pounds long before any of the boys reached that weight. Most of us were ten to twenty pounds lighter than Bernice and were frightened of her. Built like a fullback, Bernice's waist was as wide as her broad shoulders. She was well-muscled and occasionally formed her meaty hands into threatening fists whenever she felt she was about to be made the object of scorn or humor.

Bernice was a loner who wandered off by herself on the playground during recess. Her problem, and our own, arose during those gym classes when we were forced to learn how to square dance. We boys did not want to be next to Bernice, afraid of the teasing we'd receive, or that the straightening compound in Bernice's hair would rub off onto our shirts and stain them. The boy Miss Junker designated as her partner would be subjected to playground harassing until the next dance session when our teacher ordered another boy to dance with Bernice.

One time Miss Junker forgot that Jimmy Perowski had partnered with Bernice during the previous half-hour class, and put him with Bernice again. Miss Junker, a gray-haired lady who seemed to us ancient and was one of those no-nonsense teachers who could smack a ruler across the knuckles of a misbehaving student, quickly dismissed his objection. "James, you're assigned to square one. See to it you get over there right now." Poor Jimmy was near tears while the rest of us smirked.

"Bernice loves you, Perowski," one kid whispered as Jimmy, sullen, shuffled toward the first square.

"She asked Miss Junker if you could be her partner, probably forever. She wants to marry you, Perowski," someone else said.

His face flushing, angry tears spurting from his eyes, Jimmy began to attack his tormentors, an unwise decision, since he was singularly unskilled at fisticuffs. A rather small boy, David Peterson, stepped forward and knocked him down before Miss Junker intervened to rescue Jimmy. After school on the playground, Harley Woreham, our classroom bully, resumed taunting Jimmy about his "romance" with Bernice, who happened to be walking by with her younger sister. "She'll protect you from teeny-weeny David," Harley teased.

Bernice dropped her books and was all over Harley, her quick right hand pummeling him twice in the face, followed by a hard left to his gut. He sharply exhaled as he dropped to the ground. Harley got up and tried to fight back, but Bernice easily pounded through his feeble defense, punching him until he backed away, retching and crying.

Then Bernice sat down and began weeping herself, silent, great, heaving sobs racking her broad shoulders. Her sister sat next to Bernice and held her.

The next day, Harley came to school with a swollen lip, but no one asked how he'd come by it. Bernice was not in class; her sister told Miss Junker she was home sick in bed.

AT GRANT ELEMENTARY we commemorated Brotherhood Week by making crayon posters and taping them on classroom chalkboards. "In the eyes of God, we are all the same, boys and girls," Miss Junker lectured. "Brown, yellow, black, or white makes absolutely no difference. So whenever you see a child who is a different color than you are, you remember that you're no better than that child. And at this school, some children are Negroes. Does that make you better than they are?" She looked to us for an answer.

"No," we dutifully chorused. But that wasn't our reality. Except for John Potter, who excelled, the other black kids were treated differently. Bo Bean was a spindly boy, as pugilistically challenged as Jimmy Perowski. Bo defended himself with humor—jokes and comic remarks to teachers. He was considered a cutup, a discipline problem at Grant, and sometimes his wit got him pummeled by other kids. I occasionally saw him crying on the playground with some other child—boy or girl—standing nearby with a cocked fist telling Bo he'd better keep his mouth shut or there'd be more where that came from.

BROTHERHOOD WEEK was a media event in the 1940s and 1950s, and each year a member of Duluth's Junior Chamber of Commerce would be tapped to serve as the city's chairman for the programs, usually highlighted by a luncheon with a speech by a local business or religious leader. I never knew anyone who attended these luncheons, but I would read about them the next day in the newspaper. Those who purchased tickets and fostered the brotherhood concept may have believed a grave injustice was perpetrated in 1920, when three innocent black men were lynched in Duluth for an alleged rape of a white girl, but they also believed we had moved forward to the 1950s, and what did we have to do with something that took place so many years before?

Except an element of racial tension reared its head at a downtown nightclub during the late 1940s. On the cusp of national stardom, and with the hit record "Straighten Up and Fly Right" to his credit, Nat King Cole brought his trio to town for a weekend gig at Green's Crystal Terrace on Superior Street. In a few months "Mona Lisa" would catapult him to fame, but he honored his contract with the local club. Crowds sometimes tended toward the boisterous at Green's, and it happened during Cole's opening set on Friday night. Some in the audience were unaware or did not notice they were in the presence of a man whose talent ascended far beyond some run-of-the-mill cocktail piano player, and they continued joking, laughing, arguing during Cole's songs. After he finished his third number, he chided the audience: there are people here who want to listen to the music, so please do them the courtesy of settling down for the rest of the set. His admonition had a salutary effect, but there were those present, and others who heard about the incident later, who questioned the temerity of a black man who ordered white folks to shut up and sit down.

For me Brotherhood Week was only a foggy notion to which I paid scant notice. By the time I entered high school, there were very few minorities around, and I don't recall a single one in any of my classes during three years at Central High School. With the exception of Sammie McCurley, a black boy who was a year behind me in school and a football teammate, there were no black, Asian, Native, or Hispanic kids for me to feel brotherly toward. I suppose my concept of brotherhood then consisted of giving Sammie a clap on the shoulder whenever he made a nice run or caught a pass.

There was, however, one minor racial episode, worth mentioning because it occurred in front of a group of Central track athletes. During the mid- to late 1950s, each public high school in Duluth would host one or two foreign exchange students for an academic year. In 1956, our student was a Japanese kid interested in physics, chemistry, and languages. Duluth East High School received a boy from Great Britain, who also happened to be an outstanding sprinter. In the city and regional meets that spring, he captured first place in both the 100- and 220-yard sprints and anchored East's winning 440-yard relay team. The British runner led East to several championships that spring, and one of Central's coaches remarked huffily, "Why can't they send *us* a kid who can run instead of some Chink?" During the next week his remark circulated among Central athletes, usually drawing laughter.

THERE WERE FEW black professionals in Duluth during the forties and fifties. Eddie Nichols operated a catering business and served cocktails and hors d'oeuvres to wealthy citizens at receptions and soirees when he wasn't shining shoes for a living, and a large man named Jackson had a three-two beer joint on Michigan Street where blacks could gather and drink. Although possessing only a 3.2% beer license, Mr. Jackson reportedly provided whatever libation customers requested. Police left him alone; to arrest and close down Mr. Jackson meant black clientele would move to establishments frequented by whites, and who knew what problems that could lead to?

Brotherhood was a good idea though it was commonly understood that races preferred the company of their own kind. We believed that knowing those places is what made the city, indeed, the country, work for the common good of everyone. The last thing anybody wanted, after all, was trouble. And by the time I graduated from high school, Brotherhood Week barely rippled the rhythm of life in Duluth.

A LIFE INFORMED
BY A LYNCHING

THE ZEN PHILOSOPHER poses the question, If a tree falls in the forest and no one is present, does it make a sound? For students of history the question may be, If no one knows about an incident, did it happen? Can aspects of history be obliterated from collective memory?

Victors and chauvinists record official histories, sometimes leading to the omission of events that might blemish reputations of leaders and heroes. Those who challenge the historical status quo—the so-called deconstructionists—are often pilloried. Truth in certain quarters seems a bitter pill.

In the summer of 1973 I was attempting to write my first novel, which I decided to set in northern Minnesota during the aftermath of World War I. I dimly recalled my mother recounting an incident that occurred more than fifty years earlier at a location less than a mile and a half from our house. Mother said that when she was six years old, a huge mob broke into the jail in Duluth, overpowered police, removed from their cells three black men who had been accused of raping a young white woman, and hanged them. The date was June 15, 1920.

I could not remember the context of her comment because I was probably only eight or nine years old at the time. But the incident lodged in the deep recesses of my mind, resurfacing when I attempted the novel. This was a horrific story that I never heard about again, but I decided to use the Duluth lynchings for a scene in my book, with the main character as a witness.

Desiring to learn more about the tragedy, I visited the Duluth Public Library, where I hoped to find the book I assumed had been written about it many years before. The library had no such book and neither did any other library in the state, including the one at the Minnesota Historical Society.

People at library reference desks claimed never to have heard of the lynchings, a fact I also found reflected in the general public. The lynching, in the minds of most Minnesotans, had never happened. However, an employee at the St. Louis County Historical Society, located in Duluth, had heard of the incident. He learned that the society library had maintained files on the lynchings for a number of years, but at some point in the late 1930s, the research director for the society ordered the files removed. Too many students were writing classroom reports on the topic, which she thought unseemly, arguing that college and high school students should chose more edifying subjects for research.

Similarly, the clerk of court for St. Louis County claimed a judge had ordered the burning of the trial transcripts of defendants arrested for murder and rioting in the lynchings' aftermath. This would later prove false, but for years the clerk of court successfully discouraged probes by students and journalists who believed him.

For more than a half century, the lynching deniers in Minnesota held sway, and the incident was expunged or never included in official as well as informal state history publications, including the *History of Minnesota* and books about crime in Minnesota.

THE HAUNTING QUESTIONS that impelled my research were: How could such a thing have happened in Duluth, a northern city with fewer than 500 black residents out of a total population of 100,000? And why did almost no one remember or even know about it?

Finally, I opened my research with a small folder at the library of the Minnesota Historical Society in St. Paul, where I found a pamphlet describing the lynchings and a couple of news clippings from Duluth papers.

Next I searched state newspaper files and read press reports from those as well as the *New York Times,* papers in Chicago, and others throughout the country, describing what happened in Duluth the evening of June 15, 1920. I filled a spiral notebook with data and decided to abandon the novel and concentrate on chronicling the account of what happened in Duluth on a night that forever altered racial attitudes of citizens in northern Minnesota and perhaps throughout the Upper Midwest.

Because the lynch victims' innocence was not acknowledged in area newspapers, many citizens who had never encountered a black person before made stereotypical assumptions that persons of color were of low moral character and that they might be inherently criminal. Certainly we wouldn't want them living in our neighborhoods.

My search of archives, documents, and memorabilia was augmented by interviews with eyewitnesses and family members of eyewitnesses, as well as black Duluthians who recalled the incident and its impact on the lives of blacks living in northern Minnesota and northern Wisconsin. Many employees of African descent lost their jobs.

My research uncovered a few disappointments; chief among them was my learning that a man I'd worked for during my college years—a part owner of the Duluth–Superior Dukes baseball team— had been arrested by police following the lynchings. He was never brought to trial because the alleged leaders of the lynch mob were acquitted, and prosecutors believed that if the most damning evidence against those leaders could not sustain convictions, there was no point in trying others whose involvement may have been less. When contacted for an interview, my former employer refused, stating this was an issue he wished to put behind him, and he hoped I'd abandon the project, for it would serve no good while opening up old wounds. We never spoke again.

I BEGAN BOTH the writing and selling of my book in 1976 with high optimism. This harrowing, grisly story was begging to be written. New York publishers, however, thought differently. "Civil rights books are passé now," one editor told me months before *Roots* became a runaway best seller. His opinion was seconded by more than a score of others. An assistant editor wrote, "I found this story fascinating, but envision marketing problems because black people don't read books." Finally, in February 1978 I sent the manuscript to Walter Brasch, who was trying to get his fledging firm—Brasch & Brasch—off the ground. His operation was, well, small, he said, but it would rapidly expand, and my book was just what he was looking for to help establish credibility for his company.

Four months following Brasch's acceptance of the book, Robert T. Smith, a *Minneapolis Tribune* columnist, heard of my work and wrote a story, prompting other papers and a regional magazine to inquire about excerpting chapters. Publication was set for November. The ball was rolling.

November came and went. Brasch said printing bids had come in over budget, and he hoped to get a better deal.

By the time the book appeared in mid-May, most of whatever clamor some excerpts in the newspaper and magazines had generated was diminished. Brasch's advertising budget for *They Was Just Niggers* was minimal, so bookstore orders were small—one or two copies.

The title, selected by the publisher, derived from a quote in the text. Following the lynchings and imposition of martial law in Duluth, someone, perplexed by the attention the incident was receiving, remarked, "Why all this fuss? After all, they was just niggers." While certainly reflecting the attitude of many Duluthians and residents of northern Minnesota, this title was ill-conceived. Bookstore customers were too embarrassed to ask for the title if they didn't see the book displayed. And because Brasch & Brasch as a new publishing firm had little clout with book buyers, the book was relegated to shelves in regional or sociology sections of stores, where only the spine could be seen instead of the provocative cover photograph of a crowd of well-dressed citizens surrounding the victims' bodies in front of a downtown lamppost.

When the book appeared in the spring of 1979, the publisher was already in chapter 11 bankruptcy, and media largely ignored the book, though a *Minneapolis Tribune* reviewer chided me for resurrecting the incident "and rubbing our noses in it all over again."

DURING THE MONTHS leading up to publication, friends suggested I get an unlisted telephone number or prepare myself for crank calls and threats. Perhaps because the book was scarcely noticed by the public, none of this happened, though I did receive mailings from Elroy Stock, a Twin Cities businessman, whose pathetic views on race led him to anonymously send racist polemics through the mail to anyone working for racial harmony, persons of mixed-race marriages, or Caucasians who adopted other-race children. These mailings were laced with out-of-context biblical quotes and statements from pseudoscientists regarding the intellectual superiority of white Europeans. Stock's tracts derided the notion of an American melting pot, resulting in the unwholesome mixing of races, which was in contrast to the will of God.

Stock, a man of wealth, perpetuated his crusade for many years until unmasked by Twin Cities press investigations. His mailings persisted, though by court decree they were no longer anonymous.

There were several other mailings sent to me from white supremacists "proving" the multiple inferiorities of the black race and justifying the lynching of black men who had doubtless committed grave and insidious offenses. Insidious wasn't one of their words, though.

Otherwise the book received little attention and sales were disappointing. The book did not impact revisionist regional history either. The principal texts covering Minnesota history continued to omit the Duluth lynchings following the book's publication.

Eight months after *They Was Just Niggers* appeared, the publisher went into chapter 17 receivership, ending, for all intents and purposes, the life of this book. I received one partial royalty payment of $260 as the company folded and purchased new tires for the 1968 Dodge I was driving. There would be no film options, no manse with a pool, no fame let alone fortune.

But the book didn't exactly die after it disappeared from remainder bins. When politicians in Duluth wanted to build a new highway department station on the site of the long-abandoned Cook Home, which had formerly served as a residence for the indigent, protests followed. While researching the book I was told that the lynching victims (Isaac McGhie, Elmer Jackson, and Elias Clayton) had been interred there in a potters' field. It would not be right, protestors argued, to build where three innocent men were buried in unmarked graves.

At that point an administrator at the Park Hill Cemetery, owned by a local Lutheran church, revealed the bodies had always been in that cemetery, though the graves were never commemorated. In 1991 a committee raised funds, and in a solemn ceremony, markers were placed on the graves.

Several months later, the Duluth branch of the NAACP was invited to Topeka, Kansas, where Sonny Scroggins, a civil rights activist, had succeeded in getting that city to name a highway overpass the Elmer Jackson Bridge in honor of the lynch victim, a Topeka native. Within hours after the dedication, the bridge was defaced with racist graffiti.

Then in 1993 Harlin Quist called. He was on hiatus from his publishing ventures in New York and Paris, where he had produced numerous critically acclaimed, lavishly illustrated books for young readers.

Included on the roster of luminaries he published were Robert Graves, Eugène Ionesco, Edward Gorey, Mark Van Doren, and many, mostly French, illustrators who subsequently attained international eminence.

He was residing in his Duluth hometown again, he said, to care for his ailing mother, and he was looking for something to do.

With his record as a quality publisher, coupled with no other offers to give the book a second incarnation, I signed a contract with Quist.

He retitled the book *Trial by Mob*. However, this new edition of the book experienced a shorter life span than the original version. Three months later, the company Quist engaged to print the book called me and asked if I knew Quist's whereabouts. He hadn't paid the printer, his phone had been disconnected, and mail was being returned with no forwarding address listed.

I didn't have a clue. I'm told this printing made it into few bookstores outside of Duluth, and after Quist's surreptitious departure, leaving other creditors empty-handed, his nicely designed edition of *Trial by Mob* also disappeared. When Quist died a few years later, I read his extensive obituary in the *New York Times*.

The two printings of a book I once assumed might be of some consequence sold fewer than three thousand copies total, and I believed the saga was over.

FAST FORWARD TO November 1999. Sally Rubenstein, an editor with the Minnesota Historical Society Press, phoned. The press would like to bring the book back with a new design and a new title, *The Lynchings in Duluth.* My third contract was sent out and signed, and republication was slated for June 2000.

This time the reception was positive, except for another mailing from Elroy Stock, who had been in the news over a dispute regarding his $500,000 donation to Augsburg College in Minneapolis. He expected to have a campus building erected in his honor, but because his racist mailings had recently been exposed, the college refused this request. Complicated tax issues made it difficult for Augsburg to return the gift, but an appropriate course of action was taken with Stock's donation. In a fitting stroke of irony, the college designated the racist's money be used for minority student scholarships.

In 1979 people who were angered about the chronicling of Duluth's darkest hour may have had relatives who were involved in the incident and didn't want to be reminded of it—certainly not in print. Some of the principals in the story were also still alive then and could expect to be disturbed by public revelations about their activities. By 2000, it was presumed these folks had died, minimizing the sting of seeing the lynching book published once more.

In Topeka, Sonny Scroggins was busy again. He wanted to re-dedicate the Elmer Jackson Bridge and have the new edition of the book available to Topekans.

Though the city attempted to cover the ten-year-old graffiti, the racist messages have bled through. "Dead Nigger Bridge" remains visible through the swath of black paint.

Undaunted, Scroggins persuaded city hall officials to close the bridge on a busy Saturday morning for a moving rededication ceremony, and speakers representing the mayor and the governor addressed the audience. An African prince also spoke. And while the event had the trappings of a community event, few Caucasians were present. Motorists, angry at the bridge closure, shook fists and mouthed epithets at the small gathering in the center of the bridge, located within easy walking distance of the elementary school where the *Brown vs. Board of Education* lawsuit originated. But the ceremony progressed without incident.

And my hometown, Duluth, at last came to grips with the lynching and formed a standing committee, the Clayton, Jackson, McGhie Memorial Committee, to oversee not only appropriate memorials for the victims, including art and poetry, scholarship funds, and an annual march to honor the victims, but also to join ethnic and religious groups together in unity against the evils of racism.

If Duluth was once a city with collective amnesia, it is now very much a city with citizens willing to confront its past, admit its sins, and move forward in a spirit of forgiveness and togetherness. And in the process they hope to heal the city's open, unspoken wound that had festered more than eighty years.

SINCE THE REPUBLICATION OF *The Lynchings in Duluth,* I'm often asked: Why was it useful or important to dredge up this incident so many years after the fact? What good can possibly come of it now?

For a number of years I didn't have good answers, except to say that a writer is always on the lookout for stories.

But intervening years have brought certain truths to the forefront. One is that attitudes and beliefs are passed on from one generation to the next. Racism exists throughout our culture, but in the northern counties of Minnesota and Wisconsin, racism was virtually unheard of until after the 1920 hangings in Duluth, in large part because there were very few persons of color living in those areas.

Following the lynchings, however, many residents bought into the racist notions prevalent during those times. Blacks were inferior, lazy, inclined toward unlawful activities. Our great-grandparents and grandparents alive in June 1920 accepted these views and passed them to our parents who passed them on to us.

What is wrong with this is that those particular views on race were birthed by a lie. The young men who were hanged by the mob in Duluth did not rape a young white woman. But the fact of their innocence never made it into the local papers, and most citizens believed that while the lynchings may have been wrong, at least the hanged men had committed a heinous crime against an innocent young woman.

Natives of northern Minnesota and northern Wisconsin who still hold racist views might tell us they heard racist comments from older family members, and those opinions quite likely stemmed from that long-ago lynching in Duluth and the lie that black men raped a white girl on June 14, 1920.

AT A COLLEGE REUNION several years ago, a classmate I'd not seen in nearly forty years asked what incidents or events had significantly impacted my life since we'd last been in contact. My answer surprised him and also surprised me a little. I said that the June 15, 1920, lynching of three black circus workers in our Duluth hometown had tremendously influenced my life in ways both personal and political.

The impact of those horrific murders has given rise to discussions on race and racism throughout my region of the country, and I have been privileged to participate in many of them. They have been life-changing, allowing me to see and feel racism from the perspective of those most affected by it, in ways I as a person of privilege couldn't have perceived prior to the book's 2000 republication.

On talk radio, not noted for embracing civil discourse, I have heard comments deriding black victimization. Callers have argued that since slavery ended almost 150 years ago, blacks and other minorities are not only not victimized but are also granted special rights and privileges. The persecuted minority today, they argue, is white males.

Through my new friends I came to see the subtle and overt racism that I would have never noticed. An everyday act such as purchasing gasoline and a soft drink at the neighborhood convenience store may be different for persons of color than for Caucasians. Often the clerk, not wishing direct contact with the customer, will slide change back to persons of color rather than handing it to them—exchanges I never consciously observed before. Or take the case of the fifteen-year-old sophomore from a St. Paul suburban high school, who in 2004 was stopped by police thirty-seven times during the months of September and October. He was viewed suspiciously by residents and police for being present in areas where black persons rarely had been seen. The boy was traveling on foot, on his way to or from school or heading to his part-time job.

I suppose it's possible a white kid could have had similar encounters, but it's highly doubtful it would have taken thirty-seven episodes for locals to get the message.

I recall the late Jim Griffin, who at the time of his retirement was the highest-ranking African-American police officer in Minnesota—deputy chief in St. Paul—and past president of the city's school board, recounting the afternoon during his eightieth year, when he, his eighty-two-year-old wife, and his grandson, driving in a northern Twin Cities suburb, were stopped by an officer because of a faulty taillight on Griffin's car. As he reached for his identification, Mr. Griffin noticed two other squad cars pull alongside his vehicle. The officer who stopped his car had called for back-up support.

I had always thought my knowledge of American history was at least passable, but my awareness had inevitably precluded the stories of minorities and even some of the legislation that impacts them. An Ojibwe woman spoke of her 100 percent Ojibwe granddaughter who because of a 1940s act of Congress is not considered a native person and is thus not entitled to benefits accorded native peoples.

What Congress decreed was that native people must meet a "blood quota" before they can be enrolled in a tribe. The blood quota is set at one-quarter. This does not mean a person may be merely one-quarter Ojibwe, for example, but that the quarter that is Ojibwe must come from a specific band of the Ojibwe, i.e., from the White Earth or Red Lake Bands. Due to generations of intermarrying among native peoples, the woman's granddaughter does not meet the one-quarter specifications with any one band, thus she is not officially a native person. The woman said that many bands are so small that members must marry outside their band to avoid passing on recessive genes. She concluded her remarks, "What European invaders tried to do nearly three hundred years ago—to achieve the elimination of our people—is now beginning to come to pass, and almost nobody knows about it." Until she spoke, I was one of the many who didn't know.

Perhaps America will never be truly color-blind. Prejudices built over centuries are difficult to overcome. But in seminars on race and community in Wisconsin, Minnesota, and Kansas, I have encountered men and women of goodwill who do not find the task daunting. They esteem the worth of all people, quietly and steadily working toward the betterment of our communities with little or no recognition. There is no self-aggrandizement built into their motivations; they are simply people doing the right thing. And in many cases, they are going more than the extra mile.

I'm thinking of the Clayton, Jackson, McGhie Memorial Committee in Duluth—dozens of dedicated volunteers who regularly met for three years to raise funds for the establishment of a moving memorial to the lynching victims in that city and who also created a curriculum available online to any teacher who desires access to information for his or her classroom. Nearly eight years after the formation of that committee, members still organize an annual march from the former Duluth jail to the memorial site to commemorate the victims and the healing of racism in the city. So successful have their efforts been that the committee is frequently consulted by other communities seeking their own memorials for those victimized by racial injustices.

What I have learned from the aftermath of a terrible tragedy is that there are persons of boundless energy and integrity who work to make communities stronger and better. My involvement with them, made possible only because I documented the Duluth lynchings, has enriched my life and broken through my long-held cynicism, teaching me that people of goodwill matter and make a difference.

Finally, the story of the Duluth lynchings shows us that if racism can be fostered by a lie, it can be eliminated by the truth, and according to the biblical imperative, we will know the truth, and the truth will make us free.

ACKNOWLEDGMENTS

IT IS NOT POSSIBLE, I think, to write a book like *Zenith City* without acknowledging those who contributed anecdotes or information included in the text or whose emotional buttressing sustained the author through the process of completing the manuscript. I am especially indebted to those Duluthians whose presence both enriched my life and gave birth to the stories in this book. They could not have known that their mere presence, shenanigans, foibles, or friendship of thirty or forty or fifty years ago would one day surface in a book written by their old neighborhood or school chum.

Beyond my immediate family, from my boyhood gang there's Dick and the late Bruce Hassinger, Dick Graver, Larry Greenberg, and the late Dick and Dennis Gappa, Rodger Rowe, Jerry Sorenson—the kids I encountered almost daily. The neighborhood wasn't void of girls, but we paid them scant prepubescent heed.

Much of my early life was influenced by the sports teams on which I played. While not recognizing it at the time, the teams and our games insinuated themselves into my subconscious, reemerging decades later in yarns often long-forgotten by my buddies. I am indebted to those old teammates, as I am to lifelong friends developed in the Duluth Central High School class of 1957: Ron Raver, Dave Baker, Ralph Golberg, Paul Wicklund, Bill Swiler, Frank Tomars, Norm Gill, Al Merry, the late Peter Patronas, and the late Ray Karkkainen. There were college pals, too—Bill Gilchrist, Harold Segal, and I also encountered Dan Kossoff, my folk-singing partner, at the University of Minnesota–Duluth, who, with his wife Dinah, graciously hosted me in their Jacksonville, Florida, home during my treatment for prostate cancer. An added plus in our five-decade friendship, Dan likes my stories.

I remain deeply indebted to my wife, Judith, a tireless first reader, editor par excellence, and best friend, and brothers David and Stephen, who read and critiqued much of the manuscript. Over nearly four decades, I've run numerous stories and quips by my Mississippi and Rum River fishing partner, Jack Bibee. His positive responses encouraged the development of several of these essays. Fellow author Bob Lacy read and critiqued the entire manuscript during our weekly sessions at our favorite Caribou Coffee establishment. Phyllis Goldin and Wanda Brown have provided encouragement and friendship since our shared residencies at the Anderson Center for Disciplinary Studies in Red Wing, Minnesota, in the late 1990s. Barry Schreiber and Barbara Rudquist offered continual support, and Barry, professor of criminal justice at St. Cloud State University, has had me address his classes on the Duluth lynchings for more than ten years. Thanks also to Kristian Tvedten, who prepared the manuscript, and to Todd Orjala, former editor of the University of Minnesota Press, who suggested concentrating on my Duluth hometown in this collection.

PUBLICATION HISTORY

Most of the chapters in this book were previously published else-where, and I gratefully acknowledge those publications here. Some essays were revised from their original form for *Zenith City*.

"This Is Duluth!," "Uncle See-See's Secret," and "Joe DiMaggio Turns His Lonely Eyes toward the Girl at 2833 West Third Street" were first published in *Whistling Shade*.

"Beware the Ides of March," "The Hill," and "The Grand Piano Smelt" were first published in *Lake Superior Magazine*.

"He Believed Writers Are Made, Not Born," "For a Moment Dylan Played in Our Shadow," and "Remembering Satchmo" were first published in the *Christian Science Monitor*. "Remembering Satchmo" was reprinted in *America West Airlines Magazine*.

"Sinclair Lewis's Duluth" was first published in *Literary Traveler*. Quotations of Sinclair Lewis in this essay are from his *Minnesota Diary, 1942–46*, edited by George Killough (University of Idaho Press, 2000).

"Thou Shalt Not Shine" and "Jogging with James Joyce" were first published in *Minnesota Monthly*.

"My Father and the Mobster" and "A Family Informed by Pyloric Stenosis" were first published in *Knee Jerk*.

"Cousin Jean" was first published in *North Stone Review*.

"Christmas with the Klines" was first published in *Mpls. St. Paul Magazine*. It was also broadcast on Minnesota Public Radio.

"Broxie" was first published in *America West Airlines Magazine*.

"Brotherhood Week in Duluth" was first published in *Minnesota Journal of Law and Politics*.

"A Life Informed by a Lynching," developed from an essay in the newspaper and a speech delivered before the Forum, was first published in the *Los Angeles Times Book Review* and the *Forum* at the University of Wisconsin–Eau Claire.

"The Roomer" and "The Unmaking of a Missionary" are reprinted from Michael Fedo, *Chronicles of Aunt Hilma and Other East Hillside Swedes* (St. Cloud, Minn.: North Star Press, 1991).

MICHAEL FEDO is a former teacher and a freelance writer. His work has been published in the *New York Times, Christian Science Monitor, Los Angeles Times,* and *Reader's Digest,* as well as broadcast on Minnesota Public Radio, and his short stories and essays have appeared in *Minnesota Monthly, Gray's Sporting Journal, North American Review,* and *American Way.* His books include *The Lynchings in Duluth, The Man from Lake Wobegon, One Shining Season,* and Henry Wood's *A Sawdust Heart: My Vaudeville Life in Medicine and Tent Shows* (Minnesota, 2011).